When God Calls

GERRY BROWNE

SPIRITLINK
BOOKS

First published in 2021 by Spiritlink Books
An imprint of NS Books

ISBN: 978-0-9928475-1-7

We are currently seeking an agent, publisher or distributor
who would like to bring this book to a wider audience.

gerrybrownespiritualhealer@gmail.com
www.facebook.com/spiritualhealerGerryBrowne

Design & Editing: Nicola Sedgwick

Typeset in Sabon LT Pro

Printed in Ireland by SPRINT-Print

3 5 7 9 10 8 6 4

Dedication

I would like to dedicate this book to my family:
Jean, the woman who married me and whose love
saved my life on many occasions;
My children Liam, Emma, Eoin and Sarah;
and my grandchildren
Molly, Jack, Skylar-Rose, Bella, Lucy, Riley and Cara

'Life has its many gifts'

Author's Note

When God Calls is the account of how my spiritual awakening and meeting my twin flame changed my entire world. I also hope to show that no matter how hard life can be at times, things can always get better.

It was my faith and trust in God that kept me going in my darkest days, and which has brought me to where I am today.

The healing work I do involves helping people work through emotional issues and difficulties in their lives as well as giving them hands on healing. In all cases I honour client confidentiality, and where a healing story is mentioned in the book, the person's anonymity is maintained.

In addition, some names and identifying details have been changed to protect the privacy of individuals.

I hope you enjoy taking the journey with me.

Warmest wishes
Gerry

CONTENTS

CHAPTER 1

Beginnings

Even though I was christened Gerard I always felt it was important to be called Gerry. This was despite my grandmother's insistence to have me called by my full name. But I somehow knew Gerard was too severe for me and the shorter version was more gentle, fitting in better with my personality. When I grew up I learned that my name means 'God's spear'. As my life has progressed I have not doubted I was christened for the work I was going to do. My childhood determination to be named Gerry may have been a reminder that not all is ever as it seems and it is a preordained divinity that actually shapes our nature.

I was born in Dublin in 1958 and grew up in Dalkey, a village on the south side of the county. Today Dalkey is a picturesque hot spot full of cafés, restaurants, boutique shops and pubs, but back then it was just a small town on the outskirts of Dublin, blessed with two harbours and nestled in against Dalkey Hill, which boasts beautiful panoramic views.

I was the second youngest of six children, and did the normal things kids do, like exploring, getting up to mischief and fun and playing games like football, Cowboys and Indians, and Hide-and-go-seek. My adventure playground was Dalkey and Killiney Hills and their forest parks. I also roamed around Dalkey Quarry and the rocks along the seafront. Dad was a mechanic and Mum, as well as looking after all of us, worked in administration jobs and was active in the community. She helped to get the local boys' club built and was also secretary of other voluntary organisations.

When I was small I saw spirits and experienced a number of strange events. Mum told me it was all just my imagination. I now know I took my sensitivity from her, but she was afraid of her gifts, and in spite of her ability to sense and see spirits, she felt she had to deny they were there in order to protect herself and her children from the spirit world. In those days people were conditioned to believe that communicating with God, Spirit and the angels was only within the remit of the priests. When I talked to her about seeing faces in the different levels of darkness when I was in my bed at night, she said they were just shadows created by the clouds going across the sky. Of course this couldn't have been possible as my curtains were closed – and I couldn't see how clouds could have real faces – but that was Mum's last word on the subject and so I tried my best to ignore them.

I also had many night terrors and was afraid of the dark. I was scared of falling asleep because my dreams were often accompanied by sensations of great fear and of choking. When dawn came and I could see the normal world around me again

I always felt a sense of relief and peace, grateful that the night was over and I was still alive.

It seemed that all I had to do was talk about something and it would happen. But even when I had a foretelling about impending doom, I could hardly believe it myself. One time I said to Mum, 'Wouldn't it be funny if Granda died on a Thursday', which he duly did. Mum never talked to me about my prescient comments. She probably wanted to leave well enough alone. Another day I was in the car with my father and I remember commenting about how great it was running. 'Everything is going so well, Dad! You haven't even had a flat tyre.' Straight after I said this to him, we went around the next bend and Bang! The tyre blew out. Dad didn't see the humorous side of this and spoke some Irish to me, or at least that's what I thought it was at the time.

In the middle of summer one year my parents decided to take Joey, Marcus and myself, the three youngest boys in the family, on a camping holiday around Ireland. We set off on this grand expedition in an old Morris Minor called Betsy. To this day I still remember her registration plate: ZE 8773. We first visited my older brother Kevin who was in Waterford on summer camp with the FCA (Ireland's army volunteer reserve force, now disestablished), and then we set up camp in Tramore. From there we headed to Youghal and put up our tent in almost complete darkness, lit only by the headlights of the car. In the morning Mum got a fright when she saw that we had camped right on the edge of a steep slope that led down to the sea! From there we drove to Kerry, pitching our tent on the foothills of the Kerry mountains. We toured around Killarney the next day and then drove off towards Limerick, arriving in pelting rain at a small town called Abbeyfeale.

It so happened that Dad needed to turn the car around on a narrow road. But as he did, there was a loud thump as the back of the car bounced into a ditch. Dad got angry and spoke some more 'Irish' language. As he was afraid of running the risk of incurring further damage to the car if we drove on, he carefully manoeuvred the car out of the ditch and parked it on the side of the road. It was evening and the light was fading, so he said he'd wait until morning to check out the undercarriage. Dad knew when to take risks with cars and when not to.

I remember that day like it was yesterday. In the lashing rain, Dad walked to the nearest house and asked a local farmer if he could set up our tent in his field. The farmer, a kindly man, said he could do one better. He had an empty house beside his own where he said we could stay the night. We all gratefully made our way to our temporary accommodation. It was quite basic with no electricity, but nice and warm. When it got dark Mum lit a long-lasting candle she had taken with her. Then we made the beds and lay down to sleep. By now the rain had stopped and a hushed calm filled the house. It was very still and peaceful. Mum read us to sleep with a book she had about the 1916 Rising called *The Insurrection*.

In the morning Mum woke up in a panic. The candle had gone out, even though there had been plenty left to burn. There hadn't been a breeze or a draught in the house so it could not have gone out by itself.

'Who blew out the candle?' she demanded.

We all shook our heads.

'I knew it,' Mum said fearfully. 'A spirit put the candle out. I knew the place was haunted the moment I walked in the door.'

This was one of those few times when Mum did not deny spirits existed or that she could sense them around her. She was clearly frightened and wanted to leave the place as soon as possible. Dad went out to check the car. He had been concerned that the rear axle was damaged, but luckily enough, his worries were unfounded. So we all packed the car up as fast as we could and left the town as though we were on fire.

I thought it was quite a coincidence that many years later I did my first Evening with Spirit in a small holistic centre in, you've guessed it, Abbeyfeale. It was like things had come full circle – from Mum being so afraid of spirits that she rushed us out of Abbeyfeale, to her son coming back years later to talk to the local spirits. Sometimes life is stranger than fiction.

When I was young I kept praying to God that I would stop seeing spirits, because they frightened me so much. At night I often slept at the wrong end of the bed so I could see the comforting light emanating from the sitting room. On nights I could not get to sleep I'd get my brother Marcus to stay awake with me till the morning, like it was a great adventure. Poor brother, when he fell asleep I'd keep waking him up.

Years later I heard a story from a woman who had similar problems when she was a young girl. She also saw spirits at night, and was scared of them too. Her solution was to take turns watching out for the spirits with her younger sister. Her sister took the first watch and it so happened that by the time the sister who saw spirits was due to take her turn, both of them had fallen asleep peacefully! I thought, what an intelligent young girl she was.

I can see now that the thoughts I had about religion and spirituality were quite uncommon for a small child, but back then I saw them as perfectly normal. When I was in High Babies in school, about five years old, I knew there had to be past lives, but how could I balance this with the Catholic teaching the nuns were giving me? I found it hard to reconcile the belief that we only have one life, particularly with regard to the miserable lives the poor starving children in developing countries had. However, since all the grown-ups around me seemed to go along with this misconception, I said nothing and pretended to agree with them.

As time has passed, I can see how people believe it. After you die your physical body will not live on Earth again. However, your spirit has probably visited here many times in the past and may return again in the future. The Church was right in that your physical body has but one existence – but I was also right. The reason our spirits return to Earth living many different lifetimes is to give us all equal chances to encounter every aspect of the human experience. It was for me the only way life could be fair, and how I thereby trust God as a loving Father.

At school we were also taught about Limbo, a place between heaven and hell where souls were supposed to go to who had not been baptised. In my child's mind and heart I could not see a loving God dumping unbaptised infants like that. I kept thinking it was so unfair that these poor babies could be judged in this way with no real opportunity to have a life and shine their own light. Thankfully, in recent years a report was signed by the pope that effectively demoted Limbo.

In the patriarchal church where priests, nuns and other religious figures were deemed the only recognised intermediaries between God and man, any other reported communications with Spirit were considered to be dangerous and from the darkness. This was except for those rare verified cases of apparitions that happened to ordinary people like Bernadette of Lourdes and the group of local people at Knock in County Mayo. It is sad that Spirit has to work so hard to have a trusted impact on the ordinary lives of people. Maybe the clergy thought it would create fear and it would be better if ordinary people were kept in ignorance, because 'what they don't know won't hurt them'.

I remember when I was about six, Mum took me to Mass before I made my First Holy Communion. I am assuming that she was trying to prepare me for the third sacrament in a child's Catholic journey, the previous two being Baptism and Confession. At the offertory she said, 'Kneel down.' I promptly said, 'No.' She said, 'Kneel!' I said no again. Coming out of the church I thought I'd be murdered. Mum growled, 'Why wouldn't you kneel down?' I responded, 'Well, if God is my father in heaven, that means Jesus is my brother, and I won't kneel in front of one of my brothers.'

I was just relieved then that she didn't give me a clout. A smack across the head or legs for being cheeky was common back then. Apparently it was considered part of good parenting. 'This hurts me more than it does you' was the kind of blanket excuse parents and teachers gave. From my perspective as a child I remember thinking: save yourself pain then, and don't hit me.

On a number of occasions I asked Mum questions about God, heaven and the angels. I was never too concerned when she didn't know the answers, and my thoughts would soon turn to more important things like sweets or ice cream. Every Sunday we went to Mass and time and again Mum's mouth was often left hanging open when she heard, in a gospel, reading or homily, the exact answer to one or other of the questions I would have asked her. 'Did you hear that!?' she would whisper to me. 'God gave you the answer to your question!' As I would have invariably forgotten about whatever question I'd asked Mum, I didn't pay much attention to her exclamations – but she was left wondering and amazed.

Eventually my prayers worked and I stopped seeing spirits and having odd adventures. I reckon I closed down spiritually at about twelve years of age. But a number of events which happened in the following years showed that my gifts had not completely gone away.

When I was around sixteen I bought a book, *Fifty Years of Psychical Research* by Harry Price. I found it a very interesting read, but then it went missing. I later found out that the book had been taken by my uncle John who was asked to dispose of it courtesy of my mum. It was another reflection of the fear she had of this type of thing, and her way of protecting me was to block my interest in Spirit as much as she could.

In my twenties, I had a job in Blackrock, a town near to where I lived. I used to visit the church there at lunchtime. Sitting in the stillness, I began to notice that the centre of my hands would tingle with the feeling of pins and needles and a burning sensation. This strange feeling would last as long as

I was in the church and became a constant companion each time I visited that place. My mind was in turmoil. I couldn't figure out what it meant. I thought maybe God was having a laugh at my expense and I used to speak silently to Him: Don't even think about giving me holes in my hands. How would I explain that to my mum or if I went out on a date! Then I wondered if I was just crazy. I was certainly not a saint, and really didn't think the stinging in my hands was anything spiritual. I never considered becoming a monk or taking holy orders; that path in life never appealed to me. My brother Marcus actually wanted to be a Franciscan monk, but never followed that dream.

One day, when I was in my late twenties, I was driving up Fortunestown Lane, a narrow winding road in Tallaght. Suddenly I heard a voice which told me to slow down and pull in. As I instinctively obeyed, a white van came round the corner and smashed into my car. If I hadn't listened to that voice it was definitely a day I could have been given my wings.

It was only some hours later that I realised that I had been unaware of the time that had actually elapsed, from the moment the accident took place to the moment I re-awoke in my car and heard a garda (Irish police officer) telling me that an ambulance had arrived. As far as I recalled I was in the car all the time and the accident had just happened. But that was not the case. The truth was, a local resident who had seen the crash took me into his home and minded me till the police arrived, and when a garda put me back into my car it was then I came to. I believe that the shock of the accident separated me from my spirit and I had an out-of-body experience – and it was only when I was put back into the car that my physical and spiritual being rejoined.

To this day I don't know why the garda put me back in the driving seat of my car. I often wonder what would have happened if he hadn't brought me back to the vehicle. Would it have been possible that I would have stayed detached and a part of my spirit would have remained split off at the site of the accident? The car was a write-off except for the driving seat, and I was very lucky not to have been seriously injured. I just had a bad concussion and a sore wrist from hitting it against the gearstick. But apart from that, not even a cut or a bruise. The other driver suffered just minor injuries as well. I don't know what condition his van was in, but I would imagine it was as badly damaged as mine was. Unfortunately I don't remember who the person was who helped me that day, or the kindness I received from that caring human being, but what gave me great comfort was the knowledge that there are good people everywhere who help others when least expected.

I was twenty-eight when my dad died. That morning I was in Pearse Street and I saw an ambulance flying up out of the docks where Dad worked. In my head I suddenly heard the words, *That's Dad*. To this day I don't know whether Dad was in that ambulance or if it was a warning from Spirit. When I arrived home less than an hour later, I heard that Dad had a massive heart attack and had died. He had gone to work that morning and had just dropped dead. He was sixty-three.

Ten years later, when I was thirty-eight, my brother Joey died suddenly of a heart attack. On the morning of his passing I was driving up by Marley Park, near to where he lived. I used to frequently visit him to have a chat and a cup of tea. On this occasion, I considered calling over but because I had a lot on that day I thought I would just go on home. After driving for another twenty minutes or so, out of nowhere I heard a voice which said: *You are going to go home and find out something you won't like. There is nothing you can do about it, so get on with life.* I arrived home to see my wife at the door, waiting for me. She told me my brother had just passed. My whole life changed that day. I lost a brother who had minded me and looked after me all his life. We had gone to school together, played and fought with each other, and had worked together. And now he was gone, just like that. His loss affected me profoundly.

Almost two years later, the day before Valentine's Day, my brother Johnny came up from Drogheda, where he lived, to visit the family in Dublin. The only one of us he didn't meet was Kevin, the oldest boy, who was away at the time. On the day, he met everyone else including my sister. Johnny had previously called me and asked me to come over but I had been working long hours that day and was tired by the time I came home. I told him I would catch up with him the next time he was up. Later that evening Johnny went up to the local pub with Mum and my younger brother, Marcus. Johnny rang me again to join them for a drink. I really didn't feel inclined to go but he kept asking me to come along.

Finally, I gave in, got in the car and drove to the pub he said they were in. But typical! None of them were there. It was obvious they had gone on to another pub, but as they hadn't told me where they were and I didn't want to go looking for them, I decided to go to Mum's house and wait on them all to return home. Even though I had a key to the house, I instinctively knocked on the door. To my surprise, Johnny answered. He told me he had wanted to come home early from the pub because he was not feeling well. We went into the kitchen and he asked me to make him a cuppa. Sitting at the table, I thought he didn't look good at all, but he said he'd be fine once he had a cup of tea.

As I put the kettle on, I had a deep intuition that it was important to get him checked out in the hospital. After Joey's death two years before, and the fact that Dad had also died from a heart attack, I didn't want to take any risks with Johnny. 'Get in the car,' I told him. 'We're going to St Michael's.' This is a hospital in Dun Laoghaire, a town just a couple of miles down the road.

Johnny complied without argument. We got into my car, and I started driving. I was not expecting what happened a few minutes later. Outside Teddy's ice cream shop, near the People's Park in Dun Laoghaire, Johnny suffered a massive heart attack. Suddenly a peace you could cut with a knife engulfed the car and it stretched out all around us. It somehow felt like we were being protected. Unaccountably, I felt very calm.

Reassuring Johnny as best I could, I drove to Accident and Emergency at the back of the hospital, about five minutes further on. I wasn't speeding or crashing lights or anything, yet a driver in front of me automatically pulled over to let me pass. Somehow he knew he had to get out of the way; it was like the angels were clearing a path for me. When we arrived at the hospital Johnny was attended to straight away, but it was too late. He passed away. Waiting in the hospital corridor, I saw a picture of Our Lady hanging on the wall. I looked up at it and said, 'Mary, there is nothing I can do for him now. He's in your hands. Look after him for me.' It was only later I appreciated the faith I had in that moment. Whether he lived or died, I knew my brother would be safe.

I know now, all these years later, even though Johnny wasn't consciously aware of it himself, he had actually come up to say goodbye to all the family in Dublin. Everyone, that is, except Kevin. Both Johnny and Kevin were really close, and I think Johnny wouldn't have wanted Kevin to be in the middle of all the drama that happened that evening. Spiritually, I believe he was minding Kevin, his Irish twin. 'Irish twins' is a phrase, rarely used these days, that describes two children who are born within a year of each other.

Nothing else out of the ordinary happened for another four years. Little did I realise that the doors to my spiritual gifts, closed for so long, would then be flung open, and my life would be changed forever.

CHAPTER 2

The Circus Comes to Town

Up until I was forced to face my true path, I was living a pretty normal life. I was married and a father of four children, two boys and two girls, living on the south side of Dublin. I was self-employed, working in sales and marketing. I had fallen in love with Jean, my future wife, at first sight, with signs that made it clear we would marry. You could say it was written in the stars. My aunt and uncle were her godparents, my grandfather and her grandfather worked on the buses together, and I had worked with her brother for a few years as a young boy.

My awakening was very much a shock and it came out of nowhere. It was like a part of my spirit had been sleeping and some little angel had set the alarm clock for July 2002. As it went off I embarked on a scary, amazing, strange, fantastic, destructive journey, not having a clue where it would lead me.

Two birthdays and a funeral intertwined were going to help take me out of my normal existence. Vera, a good friend of

14

my wife, invited us to her son Robert's 21st birthday party on a weekend in July. My niece was also celebrating her 21st around the same time, and had arranged a family get-together in a Chinese restaurant in Kill of the Grange, a neighbourhood near the suburb of Foxrock, the following week. Jean and I looked forward to attending both festivities.

We went to the first 21st where Roger was happy to be celebrating his coming of age. We all ate, drank, sang and danced. However, an odd feeling overcame me that evening. My attention kept being drawn to Roger's father, John, a man in his forties. The phrase, *He is in real trouble*, ran incessantly through my brain all night. I could not take my eyes off him. Occasionally he'd catch me staring. I'd avert my gaze but soon my eyes were right on him again. Towards the end of the night John came over and hovered beside me. He knew I'd been looking at him and I sensed he wanted to ask me what was up. But the moment passed, and nothing was said. Soon after that, the party came to an end.

The night after the party I was kept awake by spirits for the first time in years, and over the next couple of days I started to notice long-forgotten things from my childhood and some new things too. I saw faces in the various shades of darkness and shadowy movements in the house, and heard noises which included creakings in floorboards I'd never heard in my home before, and disembodied voices in the night. I became restless and uneasy with these disturbances.

A few days later John, Roger's father, died unexpectedly. I felt sick. I had a vague recollection that this strange knowing of when people would die had happened to me when I was a child, but my blocked memory had forgotten about it up to now. I knew there was something familiar to all this but didn't want to dig deeper. However, the date in the Chinese restaurant with my brother Kevin's family was going to crank up things just a little bit more.

But before this event, Jean and I called to see John laid out in his home. Unusually for Dublin, he was waked in his own house and to see him there threw me back to remembering my own brother of the same name and age who had died in the car beside me in Dun Laoghaire. He too had been waked at home. I tried to numb myself like I had done before at the sad and painful family funerals I had been to over the years. But this time it didn't work, and I was fully aware of the pain within me.

After paying Vera and her family our respects we headed off to the restaurant, not in a very celebratory mood. However, we had to try to be upbeat for a little while. We had experienced death but my niece was celebrating life. The meal was lovely in the restaurant that night and pleasant conversations were shared with good people. Within this gentleness and warm atmosphere our mood started to lift. In the corner sat Trisha and next to her, Pam. They were special friends and friends of my sister-in-law. Pam had been her childhood pal and had grown up on the same road in one of Dublin's more leafy suburbs. Pam was also godmother to my niece. I had met her occasionally before, but being ten years younger I had little in common with her so we didn't talk much. At the end of the meal another sister-in-law of mine started to read Trisha's tea leaves.

'Here,' I said. 'Give me the teacup. I've been to enough psychics over the years. I should know exactly what to do.' I wanted to have a bit of a laugh. As I proceeded to read the tea leaves, saying whatever came into my head, Pam said, 'You're not making that up! You are intuiting that.'

As Pam looked me in the eyes I saw she serious. She really believed I was giving an accurate reading. I was a little panicked and didn't know what to think, so pushed the cup back across the table really fast. There were enough weird things happening at the moment, and I didn't want any more! So the tea leaf reading ended nearly as quickly as it began and we resumed normal conversation. I found Trisha easy to talk to, but felt Pam was quite aloof.

After a while we went into the local pub to continue the celebrations and I told Trisha about the things that had recently happened to me. She listened avidly and told me, 'You should train in Reiki. Pam teaches it, if you're interested.'

Pam commented quite sharply, 'He'd have to do his own work first.'

At this stage I had no idea what Pam meant. All I knew was that it seemed to be a very judgemental comment, like I was not good enough, that there was something wrong with me. I was unimpressed with her and thought, Yeah right, who is she talking to? The cheek of her. She didn't know me or me her. I wasn't particularly interested in getting to know her anyhow. After all, I saw her as a snob. As I was growing up I had become a reverse snob because my Mum was inclined towards being of that ilk and I didn't want to behave the same way as she did at times. I supposed you could say I was occasionally a bit of a brat.

Kevin interrupted, hearing that Pam had been suggested to me by Trisha as a Reiki healer and teacher. He said, 'You should go to Pam for a healing session. She is brilliant and it's lovely. You'd really like it. It's a great way of relaxing.'

But I had yet to be convinced. Pam seemed to know what she was talking about but I was not sure if I wanted to try it out, particularly as I had already felt unfairly judged by her.

The next day John's funeral took place. As well as having the same names and being around the same age, there were strong similarities between my brother John's funeral and the funeral of this recently deceased man – so much so I felt I was going through my brother's funeral all over again. Irish dance pumps were brought up to the coffin. My brother had danced with a famous Irish dance school and his jacket had been brought up at his funeral. Then at the end of the Mass they said exactly the same prayer that was said at the end of my brother's Mass. Considering that my brother's funeral was the only place I had ever heard it before, it felt like it was a real mirror of that very difficult time. I was startled and had to get out of the church for air, feeling uncomfortable and shaken. But more was to come.

The cortege headed to a cemetery at Shanganagh, just to the south of Shankill in County Dublin. My wife and I arrived at the cemetery before the hearse, as we had left the church early. When the hearse arrived at the gate I said to Jean, 'Wouldn't it be funny if he was buried beside my friend's father?' A friend of mine had buried his father in this graveyard several years before. I had not known my friend at that time so had no idea where his dad was buried. When the hearse stopped at the grave I saw that my friend's dad's grave was only three headstones away. I am sure you can understand why I was a bit rattled by all these things happening around the same time.

After talking to Trisha and Pam the previous night I decided my best course of action was to drive over to Kevin's home and see if Pam could help me with my anxieties. I knew that both she and Trisha were staying in my brother's house for a few days. I knocked on the door. Kevin and his wife were there but they said that unfortunately the two ladies had gone out. But synchronicity is amazing and when I was standing at the door who should drive up but Pam and Trisha. I told Pam of my events that morning, and a now-seemingly kinder personality said, 'You need to use some green.'

I didn't know what 'green' she was referring to, but when you are fearful and feel threatened you'll do anything to feel secure again. So I said, 'OK, tell me more.' We went into my brother's hall where she gave me a little bottle with green liquid in it. She told me it was an Aura-Soma pomander. She directed me to put a few drops on my hands, rub them together and then move my hands all around my aura, which she said was my energy field which protected my body. Using the green, she said, would cleanse my energy and put me in a protective bubble. As I followed Pam's instructions, I noticed the liquid had a really strong odour. I learned later that Aura-Soma pomanders can smell very strongly when a person really needs a particular oil.

The liquid did seem to calm me a bit and before I went to bed that night I said, All right, spirits, I am not afraid of you. And strangely, I wasn't, as in the middle of the night I saw three spirit orbs waft up and over my head and my eyes followed them without fear as they floated off and disappeared from sight. The crazy opening had begun.

∞

I learned that Pam lived on Achill Island, off the west coast of Ireland, where she had her own healing room. She also had a Reiki healing and training room in Westport, County Mayo. When I had been talking to her I said I might take a trip down to Westport to see her, so a few days later I arranged to visit her for a few sessions of Reiki healing, starting in late September. I had to wait until then as I was going to do some traditional dancing in Wales with a folk dancing group from Dublin earlier that month.

As I went through my daily life I kept asking people about this thing they called Reiki. I'd never heard of it before, and as I prided myself on being nosy, I wasn't sure how this could have passed me by till now. Everyone I asked seemed to know it existed, all said it was fabulous, but no one seemed to be able to describe exactly what it was. Life went on and the dance group rehearsed during August for going away to Wales the following month. We had a great time there and I came back rested and rejuvenated.

While in Wales, I visited a little holistic shop. I was fascinated by the smells of incense and the spiritual nature of the place. It was there I bought my very first crystal, a smoky quartz. The owner was warm and friendly and talked to me all about the stone's healing properties. This was the first crystal I bought from a healing point of view. Soon after my visit there I realised

I had already (unknowingly) been buying crystals for many years. The jewellery I bought my wife often had crystals like amethyst, emerald, ruby, garnet or diamond as part of their designs. It was like this world had been hidden in plain sight from me until then. I know a good deal more about crystals now and am aware that as well as being used in complementary medicine, a lot of minerals and crystals are also effectively used in orthodox medicine and medical devices today.

The lead-up to the Reiki sessions wasn't as eventful as the experiences I'd had around the 21st birthdays, the funeral and meeting Pam and Trisha. I felt and saw spirits but they were not bothering me as much. However, by now I knew I could not ignore what was happening to me and I made an effort to be more open. I had gone for a complementary therapy before, using hypnotherapy as a way of releasing anger that I had towards Dad. The two of us had always clashed. Those sessions went very well and had really helped me. In fact, the hypnotherapist suggested I should study therapy, and I'd looked at him as if he had two heads.

I decided to go down to Westport by train and give myself an easy day. I arrived there in plenty of time. On greeting Pam at her healing room, I found her pleasant and gentle and her energy nurturing. She was some distance away from the grumpy matron who told me if I wanted to train in Reiki I'd have to work on myself first.

The room itself had a real feeling of peace and the kind of sacred stillness that you might experience in a church. The first thing I encountered that day, as I started my healing journey, was a set of bottles containing coloured liquids that were displayed on a table. Pam said they were a healing colour therapy called the Aura-Soma Colour-Care System. Then she said, 'You are the colours that you choose,' and asked me to pick four bottles from the presentation in front of me.

I chose my bottles and Pam translated their meanings. It seemed they knew more about me than I did myself. My strengths I was not so sure about, but nothing was hidden regarding my weaknesses or the challenges in my life I had to overcome. It was as if Pam knew all about me through those bottles. The next thing I was asked to do was get up on the plinth where she worked on me energetically from head to toe. All in all, it was like I was being touched by an angel, and I felt safe, secure and very relaxed.

When the session ended Pam said, 'I see a very sad little boy looking at me.' She said he was very young, about six to eight years old. Then she suggested I should do something I thought was quite strange – but at this stage what was strange! She asked me if I had a photo of myself around this age. When I nodded, she held up a blue and pink bottle which she said was called Star Child Rescue, and told me to put the bottle on the photo when I got home. She said not to have it near me when I was going about my day-to-day activities or relaxing, as the energies of the bottle could affect me. I decided to place the bottle and the picture in the attic.

We said our farewells and I made my way back to the train station. I grabbed the train to Dublin on time and headed for home, but then there was a problem en route and it was held up for a while. In fact I was so late arriving back in Dublin it was touch and go as to whether or not I'd make my connecting bus in time. Arriving at Heuston station, I ran down the quay and by the skin of my teeth got the last bus home. I was very tired by the time I arrived in the door, but knew I had to get my childhood photo and put the Aura-Soma bottle on it. Rummaging around, I found the picture, threw the bottle on top of it, and put both on top of the stereo system in the sitting room. I completely forgot about putting it in the attic. Then I had a cup of tea and went to bed. Looking back, I suspect that the late train ensured this would happen as now I am used to everything having its own purpose.

Next morning I came downstairs and stopped when I reached the hall. My heart had suddenly started beating really fast. I must have come down the stairs too quickly, I concluded, and went off to work. That evening I was watching the telly when the palpitations came back. Then it occurred to me, maybe it was something to do with my photo and the bottle. Nah, I thought, no way. Couldn't be. Anyway, just to be on the safe side, I asked my daughter Emma to place the picture and bottle in the attic where they really should have gone in the first place. When she did, the palpitations stopped. I went up to the attic a few times over the next week or so and I found that any time I was near the picture my heart started racing. I also noticed that the pink and the blue in the bottle had started to fade. Pam had told me this might happen as healing came to me from the bottle.

On going to bed one night about a week later I found I was tossing and turning, tossing and turning. I couldn't sleep. I asked Dad in spirit for help. I just knew he was the one who could assist me, even though he and I did not have an easy relationship as he grew up in a time of 'Spare the rod and spoil the child'. He often beat me and our relationship became very fraught. That night, in a dream, I saw a cane hanging from the dresser in the house I was born in. We were there till I was about seven years old. Several days later I talked to Kevin and he reminded me that if we got ourselves in trouble we were sent to a particular shop to buy the cane we were going to be hit with. I had completely forgotten about that. This showed me that a child can often create real detachment from traumatic incidents rather than live with a painful history of hurt and fear. It's easier to forget rather than remember.

A couple of years ago while driving into Ennis with a friend I turned to her and said, with a tear in my eye, that my dad was a wonderful man. The truth was, I never thought I could forgive him. But I did. Instead of living in the pain he had created, in my heart I could see the love. I will never say what he did was right but a child has so much compassion and love in their heart that when they are heard and reclaim themselves, they can forgive everything. The peaceful heart is an open heart from where forgiveness flows.

In another of the Reiki sessions, sexual abuse came to the surface. I already knew of three instances of sexual abuse that happened to me when I was a child. They didn't happen within the family. Two of those incidents concerned two different boys in their late teens and the third was with a priest. My memories were pretty clear with the former two and I do not need to go into detail about them here. The third one I have not been able to clear up because I detached from it at the time, and the full story of that day has not returned to me yet.

I was between six and seven years old when my mum asked me to deliver butter up to a priest. I remember going up to the house with the butter, but I have very little memory of what happened during my visit there. All I recall was standing in the hall and looking at a big portrait hanging on the wall. I had been asked by the housekeeper to wait as she went to get the priest, which seems a bit odd in hindsight. Why didn't she just take the butter from me herself? The rest is a blur till I finally came out of the house, hearing the birds chirping and seeing the sun shining through the trees. I remember feeling a sense of elation, like I had been freed from something. Upon mature reflection, I think I must have been in such fear that I separated from myself to an alternate place of peace and safety for a short time.

The priest had given me two half crowns, a king's ransom to a child at that time. I don't remember him handing it to me, which shows how detached I must have been. I did the typical child thing and went to the shop, buying loads of sweets. When I came back home, my mother asked, 'Where were you?' According to Mum, I was gone a good deal longer than it should have taken to do the errand. Before I had a chance to reply, she followed up with another query, 'And where did you get all those sweets?' So I told her about going to the priest's house, and about him giving me the money, and I showed her the money I still had left over. I couldn't tell her any more because that was all I remembered.

Mum was no fool. She knew how much these sweets would have cost and was determined to investigate. She put her coat on and off she went to the priest's house. On her return Mum seemed puzzled, and told me I should never lie to a priest about my birthday. I never remembered saying that to him, and told her this. I knew Mum would surely have let me have it with the slipper or the wooden spoon if I had lied to a priest. In those days it was almost inconceivable that a crime of that magnitude would go unpunished in our home. On recalling that incident today, I think the fact that she didn't punish me meant that she didn't believe the priest's story. No more mention was made of this incident, but I was never sent up to that priest again.

One day, a long time later, I was telling my mum about doing my own self-development work and how I was dealing with the pains of the past and the hurt I experienced then. I briefly commented about being sexually abused and she shuddered, like she knew or guessed something had happened to me in the past. However, she didn't ask me for any more information and the topic of abuse was never brought up again.

I do not want in any way to denigrate the work that so many fine priests, nuns or religious people do all over the world in service of God. There have been too many people who have abused their power, but these should in no way be allowed to define our connection with our beliefs. We were all victims of this and we must all try to heal together.

Every month I went for a healing session to Westport. As the sessions progressed I grew closer and closer to seeing the magic of healing. I was changing in behaviour and each session had a touch of awakening and entertainment to it. As my third eye responded with visions, pictures and colours, I was more curious than ever. God obviously wanted me to be involved in healing and knew if nothing happened I'd get bored and switch off. Eventually I decided to go ahead with Reiki training. I was still doing all this purely for me and out of curiosity. It was to be some time before I recognised myself as someone who was called to serve, and longer to be convinced of it.

In everything and every way I am an ordinary man, and I have not any idea as to why I was chosen to do this work. The one thing for sure I know is that I had no intention of going down the road I went down, or living my life the way it turned out. As they say, when man plans, God laughs.

CHAPTER 3

Spirit in the Hotel

At this point it is worth remembering how fast things were happening: from June, when life was normal, to July, when I started to open up, to September when I started to work on myself. I went for monthly healing sessions supported by the use of my chosen bottles in the Aura-Soma system. I also did my best to balance the sessions with the commitments of being a dad, husband and running my own business.

There was a lot going on all the time. My first level of Reiki training was set up for March around St Patrick's Weekend. Little did I know what an adventure I was to have. As far as I was concerned, I was going to just learn and experience Reiki to satisfy my curiosity. I had no intention of working with it or calling myself a healer. The one thing I felt that was really reassuring about Reiki was the love and support I was getting to help me heal the pain of the past. Christ was ever-present and there were some very positive changes coming into my life as I worked with Pam and the Aura-Soma oils.

On the first day of training I drove to Westport and booked into a hotel beside the river. My first reaction to the hotel was that it was very old-worldly. It was full of antiques and had the look of a bygone era. I felt its history but also the spirits in the place. This is all I need, I thought, as I got my key at reception. I talked to Pam when I arrived at her healing room and told her the place I was staying in was haunted. The matron was back!

'We don't talk about spirits on Reiki One,' was her retort. The gentle smile had gone and the scowl of a cross teacher had returned. She obviously took this really seriously and was not about to tolerate any diversions. Great, I thought, This is going to be fun.

I was to train with a man who was hard of hearing. I pick up things quickly and found it difficult to give space to my fellow traveller. The situation of being made to have patience by circumstance was not something I was used to in my adult life, but was familiar with as a child. I was eager to learn and discover something new in this course and I wanted to have fun in this process. The trouble was, Pam reminded me of when I was a young boy in a convent school. I had not liked being taught by the nuns, with their superior and controlling attitude. God was so serious to them, which was a view I didn't share. I really wasn't happy with the prospect of having to deal with this kind of energy again and grumbled: I came to Westport for this!

I also got myself into hot water when I gave a practice Reiki healing to my fellow student. During the healing I intuited a message for the man which I passed on to him. Watching me,

Pam recognised my ability as a real gift from God, but when I suggested I might use it to tell people their future, again she growled at me. 'These gifts are to be used by you for healing, and so you can be of service. You are not a reader, you are a healer.'

In time I would come to understand what Pam was talking about, and the responsibility that came with these sacred gifts. However, it was to be a while before I truly accepted that seeing and hearing Spirit or having an inner knowing was a gift.

As the first day wore on, any romantic idea I had about the training process was fast disappearing. I was no saint, and the expectations of the training were high. As far as I could see the teachings were not practical in the real world. Included in the training were affirmations, one of which was: 'Just for today I will not be angry.' I found it difficult to accept this. If you are sitting in traffic for an hour, hear the whining of a child, incessant moaning from a colleague or friend, feel cheated, bored or depressed are you not allowed to react or express your feelings about these things? Another affirmation I found hard to swallow was: 'Live with an attitude of gratitude.' Really? You're standing at the bus stop on a wet day. A puddle is in front of you and a man in his car covers you with water as he ploughs through it. Normal people would say 'Asshole', but I was meant to be grateful! St Gerard was falling from his perch, if he had one at all.

Pam was becoming agitated at my perceived bad behaviour. For her this was sacred – and the way I acted showed I was not respecting the training. By the time the day was over I was irritated with Pam, Reiki, my journey, life, the world. Great, lads (my ever-frustrated comment to the angels), I grumbled. Thanks for that.

The world and people can be a very mixed up place. While Pam's spiritual approach had a touch of quiet and conservative religiousness about it, I felt spirituality should be expressed by living in joy and celebration. I didn't like fire and brimstone; I far preferred the idea that God was in His heaven and all was right with the world.

I had something to eat, went back to the haunted hotel, went to bed but could not sleep. Anger was pouring out of me. Not the sort of anger that an exasperating day deserved, but a real 'fuck you' type of anger. I gave serious consideration to packing my bags and leaving. But then again I'd paid for the weekend and the hotel. So what, I reasoned, I'm wasting my time anyway, I'm sure as hell not good enough for this. I felt judged again by Pam. Who was she to make me feel so inadequate? I now know that through Reiki my blocked emotions were coming to the surface, exposing my anger and lack of self-esteem.

As if to emphasise the level of anger I was in, around the middle of the night a spirit entered the room and got into bed beside me. The springs went boing, boing, boing! I was irate. Normally I would have run away as fast as I could, but instead this time I shouted at the spirit, 'I don't care who you are, just sit there, shut up and don't bother me.' And it did! Years later I was asked if the spirit was male or female. Some things you just don't want to think about.

Sometimes confirmation comes in the strangest of ways. A few years later Pam went to get her hair done in a local hair salon beside the same hotel, which was now closed. The two women chatted away and the conversation happened to turn to the spirits in the hotel. Pam's hairdresser told her that after the rooms were cleaned, the imprint of a body would often appear on a newly-made bed. This particular spirit had probably been there long before I came and certainly seemed to stay a long time after I left.

So that night I sat up in bed and, getting out a notebook and pen, tried to write down the reasons why I should proceed with the Reiki training. At first I couldn't come up with any words. Exhausted, I pleaded with God, and of course He helped. Suddenly I was able to write out the reasons why. I understood that everything was actually perfect, and things were progressing the way they were meant to. I had been setting myself up for failure, thinking God would not want me to work for Him. But I had to accept that I needed to express my gifts and fulfil my life's purpose, and I had to believe that God would help me to do that.

I fell into a deep sleep around four o'clock in the morning with the ignored spirit sleeping beside me. Then, at about eight o'clock, I was awoken by two birds on the windowsill outside flapping their wings and furiously pecking at the window. All they were short of doing was telling me to get up. Then the phone rang. It was Pam.

'I want you to come over now,' she said.

'What about breakfast?'

'Now,' she demanded.

When I arrived at the healing room she told me she had been thinking about not allowing me to continue my training.

Until then I didn't realise how angry she was with my attitude; after all, I was the victim here. For her, the training she was giving me was sacred and it was her duty to protect the other participant as well. Earlier that morning she had gone walking on Keem beach near her cottage on Achill and asked for help. As it happened she got the exact same information as I got from the other side. I would have been defensive before, but now I grinned as I told her about the encouragement I had been given from God during my rough night. I apologised and promised I would behave from then on. And so we all continued with the second day of training.

Part of the day's programme involved meditation, another new thing for me. After being given directions on quietening the mind and working with our chakras, we all sat in silence. In my meditation I had God play chicken with me. Give a guess who thought they were going to win as I opened my crown chakra and followed the light upwards. I felt I was moving towards the light faster and faster, and then I saw a ring of angels, then more light, and then another ring of angels. I kept moving faster and the light kept getting brighter. All of a sudden I realised where this was going. I was not ready to meet God just yet, so I pulled back and forced myself out of the meditation. Yikes! That was close.

It has to be understood that I had no idea what I was doing. It was Spirit who communicated with me and not the other way around. It was never about me. God frightened the life out of me. To be honest, I still thought that He was meant to work with anyone other than me. I have since learned that interaction with Spirit is a gift of the other side and not something we can do on our own. All we can do is be open and available.

Later that day, during a healing session, Pam said God had a gift for me. A Ferrari would be nice, I thought, or a Lotto win, but Pam said this gift was trust. Of course I trust God. I always had faith in Him. But in the future I was to learn that there is a big difference between faith and trust, that this was to be a long and difficult journey.

Reiki training over (you'd think), we said our goodbyes, and I headed off home. On my drive back to Dublin, I found myself diverted down lots of back roads all the way from Westport to Claremorris. After some time I got back onto the main road between Knock Airport and Tuam. Then I saw a sign that read 'Knock Shrine', which is Ireland's premier Marian shrine in Mayo, and I knew for sure I had been drawn there by Spirit.

I stopped at the Shrine and went into the church. Imagine my surprise when I saw the vision I had in meditation replicated in a painting in the church, which showed a light beaming down from heaven and several circles of angels around it. Now, looking back, I see it as further confirmation that I was on the right track. At the time it was just an annoying confirmation that I was not alone and not in control.

It certainly had been an emotionally charged weekend. No sleep the night before I went to training, and little sleep on the first night of training, after being in bed with a spirit in a haunted hotel. And then a long drive home. I was absolutely shattered. I arrived in late, probably around eleven o'clock, and saw we had a welcome visitor, my sister-in-law. With matchsticks holding my eyes open, I joined in the conversation till about two o'clock in the morning. I knew, falling into bed, you'd probably see me next year.

But then I found myself suddenly awake at 4 a.m. bright-eyed and bushy-tailed, with a voice instructing me: *Go down to Dun Laoghaire to a car park outside Teddy's ice cream shop.* Like a petulant child, I told God I didn't want to go. But I knew I had to and, reluctantly getting up, dressed and did what I was bid.

As I sat in the car looking out to the sea I asked impatiently, Now what? But I knew I had to be still, so sat back and waited. After a while I saw bars of light break through the darkness, slowly at first, then more and more, till eventually the sun rose to a new day. And I heard: *Now that's the way healing works. Slowly shining light on the darkness pushes the darkness away to reveal a bright new dawn.*

Thanks, God, you could have just told me!

The chakra system is a network of energy centres located in the human body, and the seven main chakras play an important role in our physical, mental, emotional and spiritual health and wellbeing. Following the Reiki attunement we received during the training, we had to do a twenty-one day chakra cleanse. This involved a clearout of blockages from a different chakra every day for seven days, and then repeating the whole cleansing process twice more over the following two weeks.

If we found a blockage in a chakra we were to send healing into it and were told we might even feel the energy move. Some blockages would take time to clear out and some would clear more easily, with little more than a knowing that something was going on. We were also told we could work on the clearouts either by sitting in meditation or while we were going about our daily chores. Along with doing these exercises by ourselves, we were also invited to sit and experience the clearing that was coming directly from Spirit.

On the first round on the first day, the clearing went as follows: With the first or root chakra, which is responsible for our safety and stability, I sensed a little insecurity which was no surprise given all the changes I was dealing with. The next day I moved to the second chakra, the sacral, which is to do with emotions and self-expression, and I felt pain in my stomach for the whole day. After that was the third chakra, the solar plexus, which provides us with our personal power. Here I felt a bit of nervousness which continued for the rest of the day. My fears were easing around Spirit, but I was not sure if I liked the feeling of loss of control in my life.

Then I moved onto the fourth, the heart chakra, which is associated with unconditional love, compassion and joy. I didn't feel anything there. Travelling up to the fifth, the throat chakra, I got what felt like a throat infection which lasted for the day. It seemed to me I was getting rid of the blocks to having a voice and speaking my truth. Then I went to the sixth chakra, the third eye, also called the seat of intuition, where I experienced a stabbing pain all day. Last was the seventh chakra, the crown, the connector to the Divine, where I had a headache for the entire day. I'm sure that had something to do with my resistance to being of service.

Second time around it was a little different. This time with the root chakra, I had diarrhoea several times during the day.

Moving to the sacral, I felt happy and content, like God was in His heaven and everything was right in the world – it was as if a new and existing future was opening up before me. With the solar plexus, I had a well-deserved day off. At the heart, I found I had one, and became a bit emotional. Then I went to my throat chakra, which was sore again for the whole day. Next was the third eye, where I felt pain for the full day and could sense the presence of Spirit around me. And finally I moved to the crown, where I had a headache again for another twenty-four hour period.

Third week and last time around things changed again. On the first day the root chakra felt fine, thank God. At the sacral the next day, I experienced a churning in my stomach. The day after, my solar plexus was a little jumpy, as if I was fearful. At the heart chakra I was tearful as I found myself dealing with trapped grief about the loss of my loved ones. Then the next day my throat chakra was croaky. On the sixth day my third eye felt like it exploded open, and ultimately at the crown I had a headache yet again, which I felt could well be due again to the pressure I felt regarding what Spirit wanted of me in the future. I was very relieved when the whole clearance was over.

I also had to drink two litres of water a day, which was challenging. When Pam told me to drink that much I thought I'd drown. Twenty-one days, two litres a day! I spent a fair old time in the loo during that time. Exciting stuff this. I understood it was all about washing the toxins out of my system and so I just tried to grin and bear it.

In summary, I was impressed that each pain in each chakra lasted just one day, and the whole process flowed like clockwork.

During this time I tried to find some spiritual discipline within myself, and started meditating and taking quiet space every day. I enjoyed this new experience, and little by little I got more comfortable as Spirit started to talk to me more.

An unexpected by-product of the clearout came when I went shopping with Jean in Northside Shopping Centre, Coolock. I found myself getting redder and redder, and felt static electricity fizzing all over my body. I had to leave the centre and stand out in the air where my energy balanced out again. It was only then I remembered a casual comment in the Reiki notes which mentioned that the physical body, while adjusting to Reiki's higher vibration, can be affected by fluorescent lights. That was all I needed, after all the other pains and aches I'd recently experienced. But I did thank God for demonstrating the truth of what was going on.

At this time spirits started to visit my home nightly, and I was woken up regularly between 2 and 3 a.m. Thankfully, my fear about seeing and sensing spirits had lessened quite considerably, as over time you can used to just about anything. During the twenty-one day clearout I woke up one night to see two children standing at the end of my bed. I had no idea what to do, so just tried to ignore them and eventually went back to sleep.

The next morning I rang Pam and asked her what I should do with Mutt and Jeff. She was horrified at my attitude, and told me to have more respect for spirits. Considering I was really tired of the wake-ups and stressed as I was from the clearout, I think I did really well to keep my cool. I told Pam I was getting fed up being woken up every night. So she went away and after talking to her Reiki master she came back with a prayer the teacher had created for release of those spirits, and any other ones I might encounter in the future.

By now I had made a meditation space in the attic where all my Aura-Soma bottles were. One night I had to go up the ladder to get them because a group of spirits had come seeking help, and for this I needed some of the bottles. As my feet touched the cold hard metal I found myself acknowledging my utter weariness about the seemingly relentless visits from spirits. Of course my house had to be beside a burial ground and also not far from where a workhouse used to be long ago, and now that I was more spiritually open I was acutely aware of the many spirits that were nearby. All in all, it was a busy pathway for the dead and I was completely drained from all the activity. When I told Pam about the situation, she said, 'You can't keep working like this.' I felt that was the understatement of the year.

She consulted her Reiki master again. 'The spirits don't have a watch, you know,' was the reply she came back with. 'All you have to do is tell the spirits that you'll send them Home on two evenings during the week. Also ask Archangel Michael to clear the space and protect you so you can sleep well. Tell him you need to rest.'

I did this, and it worked. As I lay in bed at night-time, communicating with the spirits and helping them to go Home on the appointed evenings, I always asked Archangel Michael for protection. The darkness of the room would become suffused with a beautiful blue hue, letting me know that the archangel was there. After I did the work the room would become really peaceful and nurturing, and it was never long before I settled into a restful sleep. From that time, Archangel Michael became my hero, and to this day I trust in his protection and care.

I was certainly not having a typical Reiki healing journey. I was created to be a healer and a gateway to help spirits to go Home, and the speed of change within me was a real challenge. When Pam said, 'We do not talk about spirits on Reiki One', she was right. It wasn't part of that path. However, during the twenty-one day clearout I opened very fast. It was because of this Pam had to waive the normal rules and get the prayer from her Reiki master to help me deal with this sudden change.

By divine providence, if I needed help it was always there. Even if I didn't know it, I really was in safe hands. God was in charge, but at times I can tell you, I was in a bit of a tizzy and didn't know which end was up. I did hope and trust that eventually it would all settle down and I would become as calm, still and peaceful as Pam. That was something to look forward to.

CHAPTER 4

Twin Flames

My clearout ended around the beginning of April 2003. Pam was coming to Dublin, and asked me if I'd like a healing session while she was up. She said she could work in my brother's sitting room, and that way I could save myself a trip to Westport. Great idea, I thought. That was considerate of her.

On Saturday I went for the session but found Pam upset because Trisha and she had just parted. She said her emotions were running too high and maybe it would be better if we reconvened the next day. I agreed. So on Sunday morning I came over again. The room was ready and as usual Pam had created a beautiful sacred space. Up I went on the plinth, and Pam started to work on me. But after about half an hour into the session she stopped abruptly and said, 'I have to sit down. I need to think about something.' This was quite unusual for her. She had never done anything like this in a session before.

'That's fine,' I said. I needed to go to the bathroom anyhow.

But while I was there, I suddenly heard the words, *You and Pam are twin flames.* I had no idea what this message meant, but I knew it came from Spirit. When I went back into the sitting room I saw Pam still sitting reflectively on the couch. I asked her, 'Pam, what are twin flames?'

I explained I had heard these words from Spirit while in the bathroom.

She went slightly pale around the gills and told me that was why she had sat down. She had been given the same message. The fact that I been told the exact same thing separately absolutely confirmed the truth of what she had heard. At this point, neither of us knew what to do with this unprecedented information. Because of the deeply spiritual way Pam comes at things, she knew that the room was sealed to all but the Christ energy, so she was aware this information was divinely guided.

I guessed from its name twin flames had something to do with two people having a strong spiritual connection of some kind. I had heard the term 'soulmates' before, so I assumed it was something like that. Watching Pam trying to process this message, I could only imagine what was going through her head. What could Spirit be asking of her? She had been living with her friend, Trisha, for some time and a deep spiritual connection with me would be a surprise, and confusing. Furthermore, my older brother Kevin was the husband of one of her best friends since childhood and it seemed entirely impractical to me that I could have some kind of relationship with her. I was too young for her, unavailable and knew little or nothing about spirituality, whereas Pam herself was very strongly on her own spiritual path and lived in a very different world from me.

Pam had a very basic knowledge of what twin flames meant, and said she would find out more. But at that moment her stunned surprise made it difficult for her to continue the healing. Then Spirit told me to complete the healing session. When I said this to Pam, to my surprise she agreed and got up onto the healing table. Rabbit in the headlights syndrome for me then! Under normal circumstances, Pam was extremely fussy about who would work on her, and I had only done my first level of Reiki. But I used my intuition and found myself working on her like I had been doing healing all my life. I felt my energy was heightened and it was a beautiful session in a room full of peace, sacredness and mystery.

After the healing, we chatted a little more and then I left to go home. I have to say, ignorance is bliss. I had no idea what was ahead of me. In fairness, I don't think Pam had either, but she understood how to trust and believed that the divine plan would be revealed in God's own good time. I wasn't sure there was one. On a bad day I saw my spirit guides as drunken bowsies determined to disrupt my own plans, and on a good day I thought very positively about them and was intensely curious and keen to know everything I could about spirituality.

The next day Pam set off back to Achill. As she came out of my brother's estate, buses, cars and trucks conspired to push her over to the wrong lane and in the direction of where I lived. She rang me and asked me to meet her for a moment. I said I was working in Bayview and told her where she could catch up with me. She went to the wrong place, an area called Rathsallagh, so I came round to her. When we met she wanted to talk more about twin flames but I was preoccupied with work. We had a weird conversation. She told me she had a really uneasy night and couldn't stop dreaming. I had slept fine. She also said she liked me. I said I liked her too, but had to get back to what I was doing.

'Of course,' she said, and we both went our separate ways. I thought it was all a bit strange but soon the busyness of the day took over and I thought no more of it. Unbeknownst to me, Pam called into her Reiki master to see if she could learn more. The Reiki master confirmed to Pam something she knew already, that it was true: Pam and I were and always would be twin flames.

On Tuesday afternoon I rang Pam to check on something. She said to me she had been told by Spirit I was coming to Achill on Thursday to learn about healing the land. I said, 'Pigs will fly. I'm too busy, have too much to do.'

'Well,' she said, 'If you're meant to be here you'll be here. That's the way the Divine works.'

Strangely, I wasn't able to work for the rest of the day; it was as if I was paralysed. My brain just would not focus or function properly. By evening time I gave up. I said to myself, to get it over with I'd go down to Achill early Wednesday and come home that same evening. I called Pam late on Tuesday but couldn't get her. I called her early the next morning and by five o'clock Wednesday evening Pam had about twelve missed calls and voicemails on her phone. I was really frustrated. But guess what? I *was* going to go down to Achill on Thursday. It turned out Pam had her phone turned off, as she'd had a full day working in her role as a teacher. God had made it clear He was in charge, not me, no matter how much I tried to control things.

On Thursday I set off for Achill at crack of dawn with the intention that the earlier I travelled the sooner I would get home that evening. When I got to Achill Sound, I thought I had reached Pam's place. But no, it was another half hour to Keel, where Pam lived. Wow, this place is very far out, I mused. I arrived at a very clean and tidy little cottage which had about it a great sense of peace and tranquillity. Pam greeted me warmly and gave me a tour around, which included seeing her healing room which was immaculately clean and looked very comfortable. Pam and I talked for a while and had a cup of tea before we went to work. The intention was to let the day unfold in whatever way it was meant to.-

We went into a guided deep meditation. By now I had grown accustomed to meditation, and the experience of Spirit. As we went into the stillness we could feel the energy building around us. After a while Pam and I opened our eyes. The room had filled with an energy of almost an opaque quality, and we were amazed when we saw three large overlapping circles about three feet in diameter in front of us. We had a knowing that one was Pam's, one was mine and the circle above and between the other two was the powerful merger of the twin flame energy. We sat and gazed at the circles moving before our eyes. All we could do was marvel at what we were looking at. Eventually the circles faded away and we completed the meditation.

After that, Pam and I just surrendered and trusted, and it became clear that my one-day visit was going to take longer. Ultimately it was going to last from that Thursday to Sunday evening, and to be a weekend that would set the tone for the future.

Those four days on Achill were very much about healing. First I'd be on the plinth, then Pam. There were no secrets; it was like our souls became bare and none of our histories lay hidden from the other. Most sessions lasted between two and three hours, followed by a break. Over the weekend we gave each other two healings a day. During the breaks, Pam showed me her island. At one stage, she and I walked along Keel beach in misty rain. Holding her sandals, I saw this fifty-four year old lady paddle in the sea as the waves crashed to shore.

'What a nut she is!' I thought, but then I started to feel it was me who had a problem. When did I lose the ability to be as free as a playful child? So I took off my shoes and walked in the sea as well. The brat in Pam came out as she splashed me. Then I splashed back. After a while we travelled onto Keem Bay (there are both Keel and Keem Bays on Achill) and repeated the process. Laughing and wet to the skin, we headed back to the car. Two tourists who happened to be walking towards the beach asked us was it warm in the sea. We said no. I'm sure they thought we were crazy.

When we got back to the cottage, Pam left me for a while to do a few chores. As I sat in the stillness I started to hear a choir singing. I thought there was a radio left on somewhere, so I checked the rooms. But no, there was no radio or telly anywhere that was broadcasting music. A bemused Pam asked what was going on. I said that I heard singing.

'Ah,' she said, 'Those are the angels singing.'

I went outside and walked around the house to see if the noise was wafting in from some external source. It wasn't.

I wondered what was going to come next. Angels singing, who would have believed it?

With all that was going on, Pam and I seemed comfortable with each other. It was easy to see her spirituality. It was alive and vibrant and free. As far as I was concerned, it was still all a mystery that was happening before my very eyes.

During the second evening a male spirit appeared into the room, asking to go Home. When I tried to ignore him, he gave me a little tap on the arm. It didn't hurt me at all, but did show me he really wanted to go Home here and now, please! So I obliged, said the prayer and sent him on his way. There was never a dull moment in the world I was now living in.

As well as the healing sessions, Pam and I got to sit and meditate and invite God to come to us in the serene stillness of the place. Pam's connection to the Divine was gentle and respectful; mine was mixed, and I tended to confront and question Spirit quite a bit. I later found out that in the Old Testament God seemed to like those who challenged Him. I could resonate with this, as I frequently challenged my own father in many ways over the years.

Pam had a set of special Egyptian oils, with a different oil for each of the chakras. Their aromas were heavenly, and their purpose was to open and release blocks in the energy body. As the weekend came to a close I asked Pam if I could use both the quintessence set in the Aura-Soma bottles and the Egyptian oils on each of my chakras during my last healing session. I felt guided to do this. Both of these oils are different healing modalities: one set comes from the Egyptian healing tradition and the other is linked to the Jewish Hasidic tradition.

'You don't play with these,' Pam warned, and reluctantly did as I asked. It would be difficult for her to keep telling me to trust divine guidance and then go against what we were being told by Spirit. She cautioned wisely because the oils certainly had an effect on me.

What transpired from the healing was that for the next two weeks my whole body kept shaking, and I felt I was constantly experiencing a mild but irritating panic attack. It was sustained and really uncomfortable. Eventually I rang Pam to see if she could explain what was going on. She said she would ask her teacher. This person was a very spiritual lady and did some of the same type of work I would go on to do. Her gifts, like mine, included gateway work (sending spirits Home), and she relied a lot on her intuition and sensitivity. Pam's gifts were quite different. She had a lot of professional experience in counselling and psychotherapy and also had a strong religious background, having both studied and taught religion.

Her teacher said I was lifting a curse from a past life in ancient Egypt. I said I came from Dublin and I have enough problems in this lifetime. Pam ignored my complaint and relayed the information that my shakes would stop in a week, which they did. She was also told there would be further clearings of this curse in the future, until it was completely lifted. Needless to say, I waited with bated breath for these exciting events to arrive.

Through all this time I continued to have healing sessions. I spent a lot of time on Achill Island, working with my twin flame and Aura-Soma. My mind was opening more and Spirit kept giving me books to read on spirituality and holistic healing. More study!, I grumbled. Being dyslexic, I never read for pleasure, just for learning, and it would not have been one of my favourite pastimes. But there were certainly lots of new things to find out about. These included dream interpretation, pilgrimage work and walking the land for healing. The latter involved visiting sacred sites and holy wells, and clearing homes which held lingering spirits. In addition, many of the conversations between Pam and me took on an element of education.

One day, Pam gave me the gift of a crucifix and a bottle of holy water and holy oil. She told me to keep them in my car because people might ask me to pray for them. I almost laughed at the idea. I was no priest, I said. Pam just smiled and used her favourite word: trust. As usual, she was right, as a few months later when I was visiting a holy well a woman came over and asked me to pray for her sick husband and herself. All of a sudden all this was becoming a little too real.

An interesting synchronicity occurred on 22nd April 2003 at 11.11 a.m. The Aura-Soma system launched a new bottle at that time on that day. Haniel was its name. It was iridescent blue and magenta, and was created almost to the moment that Pam and I agreed to work together. The feature in the magazine that introduced Haniel also showed a painting called The Gateway. That directly related to the gift I have of being able to send earthbound spirits Home. Three pyramids were in the picture, and these connected to my Egyptian history in a past life. The painting also featured two elevens, and Pam and I are both eleven in numerology. We knew that Haniel was not created for us – the bottle was intended to bring a gift of grace into the world – but it was and remains to this day a special bottle for Pam and myself.

It was not the first time that Aura-Soma had got in on the act. During my Reiki One training, Pam said that God had given me the gift of trust. When the twin flames were brought together it united both our soul colours. Pam's Aura-Soma soul bottle was Number 11, the Chain of Flowers, clear over pink, and mine was Number 14, Wisdom in the New Aeon, clear over gold. The Trust bottle was Number 76, pink over gold, and the combined colours brought the soul bottles of the twin flames together.

In the first few days and weeks of experiencing these things, I felt quite overwhelmed and anxious about what was to come in the future. However, Pam had insisted on trust so I tried to incorporate that as best I could, and it did help.

Many times over the years I have been asked what twin flames are. I am more informed now, but still I feel that they cannot be absolutely defined, as I only have my own experience of them. The description that seems to match best is that when we were created, we were one soul. Then, with agreement in spirit, we split in two and took our own journeys through our own incarnations around the earth. Sometimes we were together and sometimes not, and every now and then we would meet up specifically to teach each other whatever we needed to learn at that point in our existence. At other times, when God needed us to do work for Him he would bring us back together again. What I do know for sure is that having been brought together in April 2003, there was no going back. The die was cast for this lifetime. Pam used to say we were good mirrors for each other, and that was how we grew. We did our very best to carry through what God wanted, but when I pass over I think I'll tell God there are easier ways of learning and growing.

∿

Writing this story sometimes makes me want to apply for a bed in a home for the bewildered. But despite how crazy they sound, my accounts are absolutely true. I know they are special and unusual, and no one was more surprised than I was when I first felt compelled to write about them. But now I am willing to share these experiences because I want to honour them – and God – in my life.

CHAPTER 5

A Visit from Vicky

Running parallel to my energetic healing journey was working with the Aura-Soma Colour-Care System. Despite many connections with insightful people and lots of learning over the years, it was not till the twin flames were brought together that I understood there was a real meaning to life, and that there actually was a divine plan. Trying to live a normal life despite the deaths of my father and two brothers, having another brother with a drink problem, and dealing with several other challenges was not easy, but at least I was surviving. The first set of bottles I picked in Aura-Soma confronted me on lots of difficult levels: letting love in, dependency issues, sexual abuse, lack of self-confidence and self-esteem.

As my awareness grew, so did my ability to make different choices. I knew I had to learn to understand myself more but the speed of change that Spirit demanded created an urgency to the way I worked on myself. On top of this, the pace of change and rate with which I was opening up was quite incredible. Pam said she never saw anyone open up as fast. Maybe when they finally got me moving forward they wanted to make sure there were no more delays. That urgency is still there today, but now it is for my clients. I may be a tad impatient working with people because I know how much the pain of the past controlled me, and I want them to be free of their own pain in their own histories.

Pam continued with the sessions and the twin flames worked together on my express proviso that God would keep me and my family together, and we would all be safe in this difficult situation. But it really was impossible to have known what God's plan was. All we could do was trust and follow where it led us on the journey. Ultimately I was to learn that this meant surrendering everything I was, and believing God would make a way where there was no way.

The first colour combination I worked with (Bottle Number 84, named Candle in the Wind) helped me to deal with issues of abuse. It started to calm me and ground me, and brought me a sense of peace. It also helped me to work with other issues I felt deeply about, like abandonment in my early childhood. Back then my dad had been ill for some time so my mother had to work. As an adult I understand this, but when I was a child I did not and suffered insecurity and loss due to their inability to be there for me then.

The second bottle (Number 41, El Dorado) helped me to understand the difference between an intellectual confirmation of ability (through education and further accumulations of knowledge like diploma and degree courses) and the God-given gifts of wisdom and creativity. It showed me I could dream larger dreams and helped me believe I could manifest them. It also led me to studying my co-dependent behaviour and helped me take more responsibility for myself.

The third bottle (Number 42, The Harvest) embodied the theme, 'As you sow so shall you reap.' It helped me look even deeper at issues of co-dependency and disempowerment, and enabled me to start believing in my own intelligence. It also helped me learn about alcoholism and the behaviour of denial. There is a conspiracy of silence that exists in communities and families regarding this. 'If I don't see it, it's not happening.' It enabled me to see the root causes of the problems that I faced from childhood up to the present day, and showed me if I could heal them, clear them and be more aware, I could live a more meaningful and productive life. I also learned how to break old limiting patterns of behaviour and belief so I could live in a freer, happier and healthier way.

The fourth and last bottle (Number 14, Wisdom in the New Aeon) reminded me of the creative and intelligent child that had been hidden by life's hardships. It helped me to see I had wisdom and that I could find balance and harmony in life. As well as that it opened up my thinking to be so much more responsible, focused and clear in everything I did.

As I finished the last bottle in the sequence, Pam suggested that I put myself in a healing chamber of light with Jesus Christ in charge of the chamber. By now I was sort of used to the crazy stuff, so that night I did put myself in this chamber, and eventually fell asleep. I woke up at four o'clock in the morning and remembering the healing chamber I thought, what a waste of time: I had received no insights or reactions. After I got back into bed I fell asleep and had a dream. In this dream I received a visit from Vicky Wall who, along with Mike Booth, started the Aura-Soma Colour-Care System. She was dressed in coral from head to toe, wearing a fur hat, long coat, gloves and muffler.

When I awoke the next day I knew the next bottle I had to use was an Aura-Soma bottle that was coral when shaken. All day I tried to figure out which bottle it was. I looked up the books I had but couldn't find it anywhere. For some reason I could not let this go. Later in the day I was driving on a road near my house and shouted out in pure frustration, 'It's all right giving me the colour, you could have given me the number of the bottle.' Straight away *Number 61!* was shouted back at me. To be honest, at this stage I was no longer surprised when Spirit communicated with me. Later, after acquiring the bottle, I read about it. Its name was Sanat Kumara, and was exactly what I needed just then. It was to do with working on the parental balance of the male and female which had not been present in my childhood.

A few nights after I finished applying the oils in this bottle as directed, I had another dream where Vicky showed me the next one to use. It was Number 9, The Crystal Cave within the Heart. When I first started to use this bottle I received telling information about myself from Spirit. Unbeknownst to myself I had a tendency to tell a few white lies now and again. I was also prone to jealousy on the odd occasion, and gossiped a little. There used to be an old Irish joke about a man who was walking along the road talking to a friend. He said, 'I don't drink, I don't curse and I don't smoke.' Then all of a sudden, he said, 'Feck it! I left my pipe in the bar.' Well, I felt a little like him as I sheepishly recognised the behaviours I needed to work on.

The oil from this bottle was to be spread over the heart and the throat, and the reaction I had was that my throat filled up with gunge and then cleared out. I finished the bottle after about two weeks, but the clearout kept happening one day a month for the next year. I distinctly remember the night the clearout ended. I was in bed and suddenly felt a spiral of energy running through my physical heart. I immediately knew the process was complete and my heart was finally open.

In contrast to how I felt about approaching Reiki One, I very much looked forward to heading to Achill for Reiki Two. I was moving away from the fear that initially had me in a tizzy after the first course, and was getting closer to meditating properly. It didn't matter whether or not I really wanted to do this work: it was what it was, and I had to get on with it. It was now June, less than twelve months since it all started. I still had little intention of working on other people. All this was still just for me so I could reclaim myself, help spirits to cross over (so that when they visited they didn't stay too long), understand a little more about my spirituality, heal my past and live a better life.

Then I thought about my mum. Although she always denied she was able to see or sense spirits, it was clear she did. I remembered the candle incident at Abbeyfeale, and another time many years later when she said she saw my brother Joey's spirit in the sitting room after he had died. Now here I was, my life taken over, and my spiritual doors opening up. The realisation dawned on me that I was taking on the role my mother had not accepted. It stood to reason that if I didn't take on this role, one of my children might have to. I did not wish this on them because even though it had been less than a year since I started working on myself and learning how to use my gifts, it had already been very tough going at times.

Pam had become a really good friend and ally, and we were working well together. This involved supporting each other emotionally and spiritually, meditating and channelling from Spirit, and allowing our journey as twin flames to evolve. Spiritually, we were quite different, expressing our faith and love of God in our own ways, but both of us came from a strong belief in Christ.

Even though I was challenged by Pam, I trusted her as far as I would trust anyone other than Jean at that time, and accepted the growth in connection between us on a mental, spiritual and emotional level. These days, when I went over to the West to work with her, instead of staying in a hotel, I stayed with her on Achill.

I couldn't say, however, that everything was easy. At this point in time it was conditional trust and a blend of fear and excitement that kept me at the table. The fact that Pam lived in Achill and I lived in Dublin made working together more difficult, and arranging time together meant we had to work around our other commitments. But we met, prayed and talked together whenever we could. We also meditated and channelled, listening for God's words. Pam always regarded her communications with the Divine as sacred and I was always confrontational and grouchy. I was like a doubting

Thomas. But ultimately I was connecting with the Divine, even if I was dragging my heels. 'Prove that this is real, God,' I constantly demanded. Through it all Pam remained strong and committed and when I was wilting she always had the trump card. 'Trust, Gerry, trust. Let God guide us. He will show us where to go and what to do next.' I would have liked a more definite direction with a clarity of outcome, but there was none. All we could do was listen and follow.

Since I was a child I always had a very strong faith. I always believed God and the angels were real. I never believed that my plan mattered more than His but trusting that even the bad stuff was for my highest good and was somehow going to develop me was hard to swallow. I was actually afraid of what God wanted of me, but I was equally afraid of letting Him down. I suppose I was like a kid in school, and sometimes resented that I felt powerless and it was God who was in control. I might just throw a tantrum but just as in school I accepted the reality that I needed to learn and grow.

Reiki Two took place in Pam's healing room in Westport. I had a different trainee with me this time. She was a very spiritual lady who had been a nun for many years. She was bright, bubbly and passionate. Pam and she had a great connection. The training was far more relaxed than Reiki One, and I was better behaved.

It seemed to be OK to acknowledge I was a sensitive in Reiki Two. After all, this level was about working on emotions. It also included some gateway work, helping spirits and other energetic forms to find peace. The result of our hard work and diligence resulted in a peaceful and beautiful weekend.

One incident of note happened when it was the students' turn to give healing to Pam. I was told by Spirit to take the yellow Aura-Soma pomander and put this oil on Pam's feet. In my head I argued with Spirit that yellow was for the solar plexus. This argument went on for about fifteen minutes. The next thing I saw was my fellow student walking down to where the bottles were, picking up the yellow pomander and placing the oil on Pam's feet. I asked her why she did that and she said she was told to. This was a clear message: Gerry, do what you are told. I guess nuns learn obedience better than bolshie little schoolboys.

After a very pleasant weekend, I headed home. I had been buying a few different Aura-Soma pomanders and quintessence bottles from Pam's stock for personal use, and this time I bought the green pomander (The Therapist bottle), the same one Pam had advised me to use months before to protect me from spirits and ensure my space was secure.

Driving through County Roscommon I became disorientated on a road that I knew well and had driven on frequently in the past. Everything felt unfamiliar and I was confused. I came to a crossroads and was relieved when I recognised a road that would bring me into Roscommon town. I parked up at the railway station, and rang Pam to see if she could help. I told her I was disorientated, and she advised me to cleanse my energy field with the oil from the bottle I had just bought. There really was no mistake that Spirit had guided me to buy that particular bottle on that day. It smelled really pungent, and I remembered this often happened when someone urgently needed an Aura-Soma oil. My confusion cleared immediately, and I found my way home easily and peacefully. I was beginning to have real respect for the effects of these bottles.

I wasn't looking forward to another clearout, the drinking of two litres of water a day and the chakras clearing out on an emotional level for the next twenty-one days. As expected I went through many different emotions, depending on which chakra took centre stage: from peace and joy to anger, frustration and grief.

When I was a child I had prayed to God to stop me from seeing spirits because I was so fearful of them. My prayers had been answered and even though I experienced spirit activity in my adult life, I ignored it until I was reawakened. I began to have a realisation that I was still pretty connected to my fear, and therefore was not free and open enough. When I got up to go to the bathroom at night I'd put on the light because I was scared of what I might bump into in the dark.

I know that when I saw Mutt and Jeff after Reiki One training I wasn't frightened, but that was because I didn't think of them as spirits at the time. I saw them as lost children, and no threat to me. But now it was time to resolve this issue properly and accept my gifts, so I asked God if I could see a spirit. I used a powerful process called 'cutting the ties' to break my link with the fear, and asked God for assistance. As a rule this process works well and as long as the request is in line with divine will He will grant it.

Not long after this I was asleep one night, and was awakened by palpitations in my heart. I opened my eyes and saw a spirit sitting beside me on the bed no more than two feet away. By its stature and form I could see it was a female spirit. I checked to see if I was awake by giving myself a good shake. Then I thought that if I moved forward I could bop heads with the spirit, as she was sitting very close to me on the bed. However, I quickly changed my mind as in hindsight this didn't seem like a good idea! So instead I moved backwards away from it. As I did so the spirit faded. I moved forward again, and the spirit's image became clearer once more. I said to it: 'You are a spirit.' With that, the spirit vanished and the palpitations stopped. I understood then and there that spirits don't intend to frighten us. I can only go by own experience on this, but I do absolutely believe we are protected, and if God is present and trusted, we are always safe. This trust and faith has always proved my best protection.

Sometimes, though, with so much going on spiritually in my home, I had to remember that a boot is just a boot is just a boot! One night I heard a noise out on the landing. It sounded like a spirit with a bad limp. I got up to check it out. Nothing. I couldn't feel any spirit energy in the house at all, and was puzzled. I checked the kids, who all seemed to be fast asleep. Back to bed I went.

Then I heard it again: thump, thump, thump. Back up I got from bed and repeated the same routine. The kids were so angelic-looking as they slept. I even went over to my youngest, Sarah, and whispered her name. No answer, she was in the land of Nod. I returned to bed again. But when I heard the sound a third time and got up to investigate, this time the noise led me down the stairs and into the sitting room.

To all intents and purposes a spirit had switched on the lights and turned on the telly. As I stood there in amazement in came my wife, who had followed me downstairs. It was she who saw Sarah in her pyjamas hiding behind the chair. She was wearing a boot on one of her feet. When she realised she had been spotted she came out from behind the chair. I asked her what had happened. She said she had wanted to sneak downstairs and look at the telly. She had nearly been caught twice and ran back to bed each time she heard me coming. But then it seemed that she was home and dry the third time until she heard us coming down the stairs. This time she couldn't escape.

'And what are you doing wearing only one boot?' I asked.

'Why Daddy, I had only time to put on one,' she answered sweetly with a smile.

I could only smile back, and tell her to get back up to bed. As Jean and myself went back upstairs after her, I had to admit what a great job this little actress had done in pretending she was asleep, and how well and truly she had messed with her dad's head into the bargain, reminding him that not everything that goes bump in the night is a spirit.

Around the same time my eldest lad, Liam, asked a few of his mates over for a beer. As they sat comfortably in the sitting room, the telly suddenly came on. 'That's odd,' my son said. He turned the telly off, and then the telly turned itself back on. His mates were a little bit freaked, and guessed it was my son joking around. He said he wasn't and turned off the telly again. Then he put the remote in the centre of the floor. The telly came on again. Obviously spirits were bored and wanted to look at some television! Then my son said, 'Oh, it's just one of Dad's friends.' He was used to strange things happening at home.

I never asked my son how his friends reacted to his explanation. I can only suppose the beer was of more importance to the young lads than a ghost in the house!

CHAPTER 6

Greystones

It became clear that Pam and I were meant to create a healing centre together. Even before we met, Pam was given instructions to create a sacred space where fellow travellers could come for healing and support. This centre would be a sanctuary where people would be able to leave the world behind for a while, and find support on their pilgrimage towards health, peace and wellness, as well as communing with nature and God.

These journeys can be very difficult, and people on them face many challenges. The twin flames were being asked to hold a space so people could discover the beautiful beings within themselves whom God had created. Ultimately it was up to the individuals themselves to choose change – all we could do was hold the space to facilitate this development. From my own personal experience change comes slowly, one step at a time, and people need to be able to progress on their life path at their own pace.

Pam was better equipped for the journey we were taking than I was. She was better qualified, better educated, more experienced and had years of spiritual and religious service already behind her. Added to this was a life full of challenge that demanded courage and stamina. She had rheumatoid arthritis, but was determined to walk without aids, wheelchair or crutches, and to see her today still fighting fit at seventy is absolutely amazing. This typifies the strength and determination of the woman.

She does not suffer fools gladly. At the same time, she has a generous heart but no concept of limitations. For her, all was possible through God. My mum used to say that dripping water would wear away a stone and if I heard the word 'trust' once, I heard it a thousand times from Pam. The amount of times I said 'No' and 'This can't work', all I'd hear in response was 'Trust.' This kind of trust was not passive, though. It was the sort that would bring Pam from her heart home on Achill to County Wicklow on the other side of the country so she could work with me, as directed by God.

Even though she had no money and little resources, Pam moved her home to Greystones. This happened in the July of 2003, less than one year after my journey started and just three months after we were shown we were twin flames. I found it hard to keep up with the rate of change, and I was trying to come to terms with the idea of surrender and trust. Pam leaving her soul home in Achill would seem premature to some, but not to her. No way could I have shown the level of faith and trust the way she did. She moved just after I completed Reiki Level Two. Her new home would be where our healing centre would be located. The house was a fairly small two-storey residence in a relatively new estate, with a small garden back and front. As soon as she moved in, she created a beautiful healing room in the downstairs sitting room. The house was arranged in such a way that it always felt calm and sacred, and was a nurturing space to all those who would go there.

Determined to fulfil her promise of service, Pam was willing to give her all, whereas I was not in that space by any means. I was insecure and unsure, and determined my family would come first. I could not see God wanting me to leave my wife and children to devote more time to working with Pam. However, at the end of the day, I wasn't sure about anything. Hadn't God torn apart the family I grew up with by taking two of my brothers in their forties, not to mention leaving their wives without husbands and their children without fathers? Pam herself had no family ties to hold her back and was free to make her own choices, without a negative impact on anyone else.

But I had to accept that there was a larger unseen plan. I knew that in spite of being unable to comprehend God's ways I had to accept them, and that there were reasons for things unfolding in certain ways. However, it was excruciatingly painful and stressful at times, and the feeling of being trapped between being a family man and following the divine will of God would see me contemplate suicide on a few occasions in the years that followed.

In that summer of 2003 I was still not prepared to surrender my old life, even if God demanded it. Little by little my world became more stressful as I tried to maintain my old life and merge the new. Pam had made it easier for us to work together by coming to Greystones but that would ultimately create more conflict for me.

By now meditation was becoming deeper and spiritual experiences were frequent. During one meditation I was given the name 'Ishmael', and so then I went looking everywhere for its significance in my life. I checked and found Ishmael in the Bible, but it had no relevance to what was going on with me then. One day in Dun Laoghaire I walked into a small holistic shop called Books Unlimited, and there it was: a book called My Ishmael. I was compelled to buy it. As I came out of the shop, I looked up I saw a huge rainbow in a cloudy sky. It was a thumbs up that I had found my Ishmael!

It turned out that the book was important in that it connected me to a past life that I had in Egypt. The story in the book had a parallel to my past life there, thus validating the information Pam and I had received during my work around Egypt. It was the essence of the story which was important and was further confirmation I was on the right path.

In another meditation I was shown Pope John Paul II's staff, but the crucifix on it was missing the figure of Jesus. I tried to find meaning to the vision as I sat there in silence. Then I went to libraries to research and see if there was such a cross in existence, but I couldn't find it anywhere. However, it wasn't long before I got my answer. One day in meditation I felt compelled to reach out and grasp my grandmother's Happy Death cross from the locker beside my bed. As I reached out, a voice suddenly shouted at me, *Leave it. Don't touch it.* I got a fright. Who was talking to me? Was it from the Light?

I didn't like being told to leave the cross alone. It felt wrong. It seemed like an age before the voice spoke again. *It's not the crucifixion that's important. It's the resurrection. Christ died for us and triumphed over death. It's a positive message of love and care, of hope and faith.* I understood then, and was grateful for this illumination. I was also in no doubt that the message came from divine source.

Before the meditation ended I was told by Spirit to have a picture painted for our future healing centre. An image of light emitting from the cross rather than a cross with Jesus crucified on it was what I had in my mind's eye, but I told God I was useless at painting. He told me to get Pam's Reiki master to do the painting, and she did. She actually created two pictures channelled from Spirit, and they travelled with the twin flames to the various different places we located to over the years. Today the paintings are hanging in my healing room in Ennis, County Clare.

When I first saw the paintings they seemed strange to me, and for a time I had difficulty understanding their meanings. I did find the first picture was a great help in holding concentration in meditation, and when I worked in the healing room on one-to-one clients the painting helped me clear my mind and focus. I understood it was about the coming of the spirit into the infant's body in the physical world, and trusting in the transmutation of negativity. It also involved the spirit having the protection of the violet flame's spiritual energy throughout its life on earth.

Regarding the second picture, its meaning was only revealed to me when I was working with a client some years later and was getting a bit frustrated because I couldn't clear one of her blocks. The picture caught my eye and a voice said, *Patience. Everyone is entitled to their own resurrection.* It reaffirmed that healings are gifts from God and are done in His time, not ours. It brought clarity to the fact that we all go through crises in our lives, learning and evolving as we do in divine timing, before we eventually go back to our Creator. In the healing room I was often reminded that people are constantly supported in the process of their lives by God, the angels and other heavenly beings.

There always seemed to be another new thing to learn as we took this crazy journey. By now I was regularly praying for the deceased and receiving visits from spirits almost on a daily basis. Any fear I had about spirits was thoroughly gone now and I always felt safe and protected by Archangel Michael and his legions of angels.

I was also sending spirits Home twice a week. This normally involved saying a particular prayer for those spirits who were fearful of moving on or had some other reason for remaining earthbound. A typical example would be some farmers who have no one to leave the land to at the end of their lives, and their spirits then stay around minding their farms and surrounding fields. They mistakenly think that by not having a natural heir they failed in their duty to pass the land down the line. They are very nervous of meeting their ancestors, as they fear their judgement, so even after death they feel a responsibility for protecting the land which they had loved. This is just their cultural belief, but it shows how dedicated and committed people can be in a belief or fear which can ultimately keep them tied to the physical world.

One of the special gifts Pam brought to this part of my journey was her great strength. I would be in a tizzy a lot of the time. Back in those early days I was more astonished than anxious about the connection I was developing with God. I had always seen Him as somewhat removed from me, but now my thoughts about Him had changed and I wouldn't have been surprised if He joined me for breakfast some morning!

Pam was unflappable and really grounded. I do think if He had knocked on her door she would have calmly showed Him into the sitting room and put on the kettle. As fearful as Mum was of her gifts, Pam was centred and secure around Spirit and the spirit world. I felt this made it OK for me to have this connection with the Divine not as an abstract concept, but as a genuine reality.

On 26th of December 2003 Pam invited my family and my brother Kevin's family to a dinner in Greystones. As it happened, this was also one of the days I was to pray for the gates to be opened for earthbound spirits so they could go Home. Usually it would take no longer than about ten to fifteen minutes to do this work. I went up to my bedroom, lit a candle, put on some sacred music, did my call-in and began praying to hold the space for spirits to go Home. After my usual ten minutes I asked could I close the gate. *No*, came the curt reply. Every five minutes after that I asked the same question, and again the same answer was given: *No*.

After half an hour I was getting frustrated. I was still not being allowed to close the gate, and Jean and the kids were all waiting impatiently downstairs. Suddenly I was drawn to turn on *Sky News*. Breaking news reported an earthquake in Iran, and initial estimates put the death toll at 20,000. That's why this was happening. I was praying for them. I realised I needed to respect their beliefs and so I asked Mohammad and Allah to help them find peace. I felt that might be the solution – but it wasn't. It was getting later and later, and the children were now getting agitated. At this stage three quarters of an hour had passed and still the answer was no. I decided to take matters into my own hands and told the angels I was going to close the gate right then. I knew *they* would not do anything to me, but Pam would kill me for being late for dinner. Added to that, my family were getting really tetchy and were fed up waiting.

So I closed the gate, ran downstairs and we all bundled into the car. It was when I reached the end of the Southern Cross road in Bray near the golf course that I heard a great booming voice across the valley courtesy of Archangel Michael. *You agreed to do this work. You do it on our terms, not on yours.* Shocked and mortified, I shrank behind the steering wheel and felt really small at letting them down. In that moment, I felt very much like a scolded little schoolboy who had stepped out of line.

We arrived at Pam's house and I knocked on her door. She welcomed us all in and after a few moments I took her aside. Still a bit shaken from the stern words I had received, I asked her if she was ever given out to by Upstairs. Before she replied I answered for her: 'No, you always do what you are told, don't you?' She just smiled.

I told her the story, and she said, 'We can open the gate later on. Could Kevin leave your family home instead of you so we could send the spirits Home together?'

'I'm sure he wouldn't mind,' I replied. 'I'll check with him.'
I asked him and he said he would but his car was full.

Pam said, 'OK then, I will leave your family home, so you
can stay here and restart the process.'

'Fine. The only thing is,' I said, 'I don't have my manual with
me. Can I borrow yours?'

She said that was no problem and went off to get it. Our
manuals were books of notes we had built up through our own
spiritual journeys. They contained prayers for working with
people in need of healing, with each manual having slightly
different information according to our own individual paths.

As Pam opened her manual to find the correct page for me a
loose page fell out. She glanced at it and commented, 'That's an
old prayer we used to use to send spirits Home.' She returned
the page to the manual somewhere at the back of the book,
and found the prayer I was using back in my own house.

Then we back to the others and we all enjoyed a lovely
dinner. At the end of the evening, when everyone was gone,
I opened the gate once more and resumed my prayers. Every
ten to fifteen minutes I asked if I could close the gate. After
nearly an hour the answer was still no. I tried to open my heart
and think of all the things that could have prevented these souls
from going Home. I asked all the angels to help. Frustrated,
I felt I could do no more.

All of a sudden I remembered Pam's old prayer. At this stage
I would have tried anything. I dug through the manual and
found the loose page. The only difference this prayer had to
what I had been saying were the words: 'I release you from
death and mass death.' After I prayed these words I was told I

could finally close the gate. Phew! Talk about being led by the nose. It took nearly two hours to find the right words to send these spirits Home, to find the prayer Spirit wanted me to use in terms of tragedy and mass death.

From then on we included this prayer in the gateway work and we taught it at all our trainings. When I think now of that earthquake and of the people who were on the ground trying to help, from those who dug through the rubble of homes and schools to the nurses and doctors who tried to save the lives of many who were injured, my two hours of prayer seem insignificant. I know I should have done what I was asked at the time without moaning.

When I eventually got home to Jean that evening, I told her what had happened. By now she was getting used to having her time with me disturbed by God, Pam and my spiritual journey. We had a cup of tea and a couple of biscuits and moved on. I was very grateful that she supported me all the way, but I did feel sorry for her and the children. It was hard for them.

These were not everyday occurrences, but they were frequent enough to disrupt our lives. My role in life had changed, and I was no longer the guy who was involved in sales, or the man who played many different roles to feed and care for his family. Now I was a spiritual healer trying to help people. But like any other worker, I still had to get up, get dressed and go to work. The fact that my work had changed just meant I did different things. All that was happening now had to become the new normal, just another day at the (new) office.

Consistently I reminded Pam that I never signed up for doing this work, and she always reminded me to keep trusting, and to stop complaining and being negative. I used to joke with Pam that I was going to take God to the European Court of Human Rights as He was constantly breaking all sorts of employment laws.

∾

I'm glad I don't need people to believe what I write in this book, but affirm there absolutely is a God, there is an afterlife, spirits do exist and there is a lot more to every human being on this planet than we'll ever know while we are here on this Earth. My book is simply bearing witness to some of what God has done in my life and to let people know it is OK to believe in what they see and feel.

Over 26,000 people died that Stephen's Day and 30,000 were injured. Sometimes in tragedies like earthquakes, tsunamis and wars, it is not easy to understand how a merciful or kind God would let these things happen. But to me now, death is not a punishment or as terrible a thing as I used to think: it is a rebirth to a Home where we all truly belong, and is the ultimate destiny for everyone, regardless of how and when we go there. God's love is very powerful and He really does hold us in the palm of His hand.

I still don't know what my spirit looks like, nor do I know the mind of God or understand the workings of the Divine. I don't need to, because trust and faith enables me to continue believing in a plan I cannot understand.

CHAPTER 7

Umbrella Requested

'Be still and know that I am God.' Psalm 46:10. Easier said than done, particularly to someone like me who wanted to be in control of his own life. Feeling like the lads on the stormy lake of Galilee while Jesus slept in the back of the boat, I had to try and surrender to God in the back of my own metaphorical boat and hope that, unlike His son, He was awake and knew where He was bringing me.

There was so much happening: my younger brother, Marcus, unable to handle the death of my other two brothers, Joey and Johnny, was drinking like a fish. This wonderfully gifted and talented young man was running aground, weighed down by grief and loss, a pain that is familiar to many people on this planet.

In my own new life of healing and service, I was learning about dependency and co-dependency issues, alcoholism, addiction, pain and hurt and translating my own personal issues and traumas into further learning. If God wanted a healer, would

He want someone who had suffered? Of course he would. It's only when you truly understand your own pain and hurt that you can feel with true compassion, having walked a mile in others' shoes. Some people detach from their pain and don't understand how others can't. When I first started working on myself I thought I had no real problems, but as I did my own work I realised I had – and lots of them. I had just put a plaster on my wounds and never dealt with the woundings. It was then that the healer started to emerge. As I became more loving and tolerant of myself, I could reach out with generosity to others more. The author of *Real Leadership*, John Addison, said, 'To see the best in others, see the best in yourself.'

Much of the criticism we aim at other people comes from our own undealt-with feelings of inadequacy, and our own deep wounding. When we are able to see our own light and celebrate it we are much more likely to see and accept the light in others, and, better still, enjoy seeing the miracle in it. They say truth will out; well, let me tell you, so too must every emotion we possess one way or another.

Darker emotions of anger, fear, jealousy and grief can control our lives without us even thinking about them. Limiting beliefs like 'I can't do it', 'I'm not good enough', 'I don't know how to receive love, I only know how to give love', can leave an incredible trail of destruction behind us. Back at my niece's birthday party, when Pam said, 'He has to do his own work first', I had no idea what she meant. I was to meet the darker side of myself time and time again as I started to deal with a complicated and painful history, and in that process I learned how to really love myself.

When God urged me to go to Dun Laoghaire early in the morning and then spoke words of wisdom as I saw the dawn breaking, I understood that I had to work on the darkness in myself to reveal the light within. Now I was letting in more light with every step forward I was taking. Between the Aura-Soma Colour-Care system, Pam's therapeutic work and Reiki healing, I was waking up. But boy, could my inner battles be intense. As I healed, I started to see a more beautiful world and real goodness in people. The world or people had not changed. I had.

Despite all the obstacles and difficulties, I wanted to learn more about the meaning of spiritual awareness. One day Pam explained the process of 'splitting off' or emotional detachment, which happens when someone doesn't want to acknowledge pain in their lives. When a catastrophic childhood event is re-experienced through the mature eyes of an adult, healing can occur and pain can be released. But because as children we cannot cope, we sometimes detach and hold onto the judgement and pain in the subconscious. This can then determine a lot of our negative behaviours later on.

The problem is, along with detaching from trauma we lose so much of the magic we have within ourselves. We live lost in this broken state until one day we reclaim who we are by healing the wounding and freeing ourselves from the past. I was soon to experience this process first-hand in myself.

Most of the time during our sessions I was alert and aware. Fully present. However, when I didn't want to deal with an issue I'd subconsciously use a defensive strategy of going into a deep sleep. It was usually a trigger question, or something

I didn't want to hear, that would switch off the light. Any respectful soul would let the baby sleep, but no, not Pam. She knew it was avoidance. She would come around to the other side of the plinth and poke me. She never let sleeping dogs lie. When I woke up she would point out that I'd fallen asleep, and repeat the same question. Over and over I would fall asleep, but every time I did she would wake me up again.

This behaviour went on for about six months. For someone who could not get to sleep at night this was amazing. Could I really be doing this subconsciously? As time rolled on, the answer became clear. Pam continued bringing me through the battle with myself. I went from falling asleep to growling, and using a different defensive strategy. I would start sentences with, 'I'm entitled to . . .' which became a catchphrase for a while. I also complained: 'I don't want to talk about this.' 'Don't go there.' 'Leave me alone.' But my twin flame knew when we would be hitting pay dirt. So when I said, 'I am entitled to . . .', she would reply, 'I thought you wanted to change.' Pam could be so annoying like that. Sometimes I'd leave a session incomplete. In those cases, Pam said I was running, and I was.

I would then toss and turn overnight, and would be back the next day to deal with the issue at hand. I lost or won many of these battles, depending on how you looked at it.

The next defensive strategy I adopted was to talk about myself in the third person. For example: 'Gerry doesn't like . . .' Pam knew this meant I was putting the pain I carried at a distance, trying another way of separating myself from the unpalatable truth of the issues that I detached from in my childhood. She let me away with it for a while, till out of the blue one day she asked me: 'Who is Gerry?' She told me I had to take ownership of my pain. I see now I often responded with anger and irritation, but that never pushed her away. She was determined to hold a space so I could heal.

The personal journey work was relentless, with Pam and I doing many healing sessions on each other. Our intention was to free our blocked energies from all the conditioning we had since our incarnation in this life and all the other lives previously. We were divinely guided in the process. Pam was used to using her professional training and spiritual gifts when doing this work, while I experienced the surprising emergence of a knowledge I never knew I had. For the first three years of being brought together, the intensity of the healing and the depth of inner reflection was incredible.

When twin flames are brought together they mirror each other constantly. It was a match made in heaven but our journey together was not going to be easy. There were ongoing struggles between us. It was like cascading down rapids with no oar and no control. Finances were always a worry for me, but Pam had total faith and trust that God would provide. I had always been brought up on an ethos of hard work and taking your future in your own hands. I often found it hard to get traction on believing that trust alone would help me get through difficulties.

But at no point could I doubt extraordinary events which were not just spiritual but also physical and mental in nature. One time I sat down to meditate. Beforehand, I discovered I had no candles left and had to use one that Pam had given me for Christmas. After putting it in the wrought iron stand at the end of my bed and lighting it I closed my eyes and relaxed. As the meditation progressed I found myself arguing with God and saying there was no such thing as twin flames. Suddenly, in my meditative state I heard spitting noises coming from the candle. Becoming immediately alert for fear of fire, I looked at the candle and saw in amazement that the flame had split in two. Before my eyes it changed back to one flame and then became two flames over and over until it changed back to a normal flame.

I had to admit this astonishing phenomenon would have sent most people a loud and clear message, but I responded to God, 'That's not that impressive. We already had that with the burning bush episode in the Bible.' It was pretty obvious I didn't want to acknowledge this sign from Spirit, but it was hard to deny when something like that happens in front of your eyes.

Another strange event happened when I was working on a client, giving him a healing. I felt a burning sensation in my pocket, and jumped up from my seated position. Did I have matches in my pocket that had somehow gone alight? I put my hand in my pocket and retrieved a battery that was searingly hot. Placing it quickly down on the ground, I realised what had happened. The high energy running through me had affected the battery and had heated it up to the point that it was burning me. I knew Spirit was doing all these things to make me see how real this all was.

I was continually intrigued by the physical nature of some of my own healing sessions. On one occasion I was lying on the plinth and the sensation I had in my belly reminded me of a boiling pot with stuff bubbling to the surface. I released about ten bubbles of energy from my stomach in that session, and could actually see it happening under my skin. I saw a swelling form and then a bubble of energy went pop!, as it released the energy. What was happening was that pain that had been buried was now coming back into my awareness so that I could finally let go of it. Pam and I were able to relate each of these bubbles to specific difficult incidents in my childhood, and then we cut ties with them and any of the resultant damage that affected how I have lived in the intervening years. I experienced this phenomenon again in a few other sessions that followed on from this one.

The incidents I experienced in childhood are common in many families. Through my healing sessions I rediscovered the story below, which had been pushed deep into my subconscious. I worked on the issue with Pam and was finally able to let it go. It concerned sibling rivalry.

As a ten year old I saw a pregnant stray cat walking along the wall of my school. I asked my Mum if I could have one of the kittens when they were born. She said no. I was crushed. Apart from not seeing a problem about how I would get my hands on one of the kittens when it was born, it was the absolute 'no' that really hurt me. Then six months later my brother Marcus accompanied Mum when she visited one of her friends. My mother's friend's cat recently had a litter of kittens and Mum gave Marcus permission to pick out one of the kittens for himself. I felt it was so unfair, and as far as I was concerned, it decided my pecking order in the family. In my pain and hurt, I assumed I was loved less than my brother.

As a parent now myself I understand it was not Mum's intention at all to hurt me, but my younger self couldn't see it that way. Events like this can impact negatively on us at the time, and can continue to affect us in a much greater way than they should as we go through life.

So as the stories of my past were released through healing, I was able to see them from a different perspective and comprehend them in a wiser way. In some instances I had to forgive my past and let go of the pain, and in others I had to just find peace and understanding of my past, and move on. I don't doubt my mother loved me, but we never had time together. She had to go out to work soon after I was born, which meant I was mostly brought up by my grandmother.

∾

Pam didn't think that you should work on anyone unless you had done a lot of your own work first. She said it was the only way you could be fully present for your client. You had to own the skeletons in your closet. They had to be wined, dined and understood. Nothing was to come between you and the work you were doing with your client. The clearer you were within yourself the better you would be as a healer. I remember saying to Pam that if ever I was to work with a woman (I was still only doing this for myself at that stage) and they started to cry or if they talked about their feminine issues I was gone, I was out of there. Pam replied and said she believed that in time I would mature. Eventually, I did.

My Reiki Masters was scheduled for November 2003. I also

wanted to do my first level of training in Aura-Soma with a teacher called Cathleen around the same time. However, at that stage I was working on clearing a lot of difficult emotional issues, and Pam warned me that at the rate of clearout I was experiencing, if I did the Reiki Masters and trained in the Aura-Soma system at the same time I would have very few friends left. As each of the training levels in both Reiki and Aura-Soma bring past hurts to the surface to be dealt with, it would be difficult to do both trainings and clearances at the same time. Reluctantly I agreed and decided to do my third level of Reiki then and leave the first level of Aura-Soma training till the next time Cathleen would be arranging it. This was to prove synchronicitous and in divine timing.

The day of my Reiki Masters came. There were two other women there to do the training as well. They were experienced holistic practitioners and used to working with people. It was a pleasant enough two days and we practised our healing on one another, combing and clearing each other's energy fields and removing the painful hurts and negative energy that no longer served us.

The women had a wonderfully gentle way of moving the energy, and of pulling off and releasing what needed to be let go of. Then one of the ladies half-jokingly but totally in earnest asked Pam for an umbrella as she could feel the energy of a client I was clearing landing in her direction. This happened because the plinth I was working at was close to this lady's plinth and in clearing my client's energy with masculine exuberance but no finesse, I had inadvertently splashed it over to where this lady was doing her own healing. After a while we had to move the two plinths further apart to give us more space to work in, and I learned to be more gentle in cleansing the energy field of a client.

Looking back, I can see that the people I trained with helped me learn patience and how to really listen. I took away from the course the knowledge that healing is a gift from God, and that everything is in His hands and will be done in His own good time. I also became aware of the sacredness of the energy we were working with. The course showed me that I had a responsibility to work tidily and gently when I combed a person's energy, and to be mindful in sending the energy where it needed to go for transmutation and transformation.

As if further proof was necessary, something amazing happened to the chakra set of Aura-Soma bottles which Pam had sitting on the fireplace in the healing room. The colour in the bottles totally changed, becoming very murky, as they transmuted the pain and hurt released from those who were worked on in the room, including Pam and myself.

The weekend over, I could now call myself a Reiki Master. Another twenty-one day clearout followed, which was this time clearance on the spiritual level. It took about a year and a half before I felt I could accept this title and the spiritual responsibility it gave me. I frequently felt not good enough, not worthy, and not capable. But what I feared most was letting Pam and God down. It took me a number of months before I did my first healing session by myself with a client outside of the training. I knew I had real trust issues and often said to Pam what she really needed was an old priest, someone more spiritual than I was.

At times in meditation or working with people and Spirit, there was no doubt God had made the right choice with me. There were moments I could be deeply spiritual. The problems only occurred when I allowed my inner negative voices to control my brain, and it was that which caused turmoil in my inner world, which then found its ready reflection in the outer world.

As I gradually grew into the title of spiritual healer I caught up with the gifts I was being asked to use. I always consider I am but a channel of these abilities, and my duty is to be available to work in service. I didn't know what I had embarked on when I started my journey but things were becoming clearer. My reward for the work I did was seeing people benefit from the healing: they started making positive changes in their lives and were becoming free of some of their old patterns of behaviour.

It is always a privilege to watch people discovering their own unique qualities and learning how to honour and love themselves. But it is still the client who makes these changes. They're the ones who are making decisions with a newfound confidence and determination to change their life. They say every master is a student, and every student teaches a master something new. I will always be grateful for the learning I received from the clients who came to work with us, for sharing their stories with us. They taught me an awful lot down the years.

Being in Greystones was both a gift and a nightmare. The level of pressure exerted on me to work on myself and then do client work with Pam meant lots of days lost from my own business, the work that paid my bills and supported my family.

Slowly but surely my income started to diminish and my stress levels rose. Pam did not think the same way. She was certain that my future lay in healing and spiritual service and my old life needed to be let go of so the divine plan could take priority. She was used to trusting what God gave her and was able to live on whatever He provided her with. She was becoming ever-present in my life – on the phone, in the healing sessions, and during trainings. We were often asked to sit in stillness and meditate together so we could receive directions from Spirit.

Jean was very understanding and supportive. She rarely complained because she knew at some level I had to do this. She didn't want to be a part of it but didn't want to stand in its way. Our love for each other was strong, but I greatly feared I would not be able to hold it together to both provide for my family and do the healing ministry.

Towards the end of the year I told Pam that this arrangement was not working out and I could not continue to work this way. I was starting to come under real financial pressure, and it was costing me and my family a lot. Things were problematic for Pam too. She had little or no income either at the time, so if my business completely collapsed we were both in real trouble. People had started to come to us for healings, but there weren't enough clients yet to pay the bills. So if someone cancelled at the last minute, that put me into a fearful place, as I had to take time off my own work to work with clients. It was quite a balancing act.

I thought that if we could find a place to work from around the Blackrock area where a lot of my day-to-day work was concentrated, it would be easier. But there was no money and no place available. Guess what! The irrepressible Pam found a house and the money for a deposit by the skin of her teeth, and just like that, Greystones was gone. Blackrock quickly became our new reality and Greystones faded into the past. To help the situation we merged our incomes as a single business to give us a chance to make things work.

It was a very hard decision to make. Little did I know then that my identity was going to be subsumed into the twin flames, my business was going to disappear and ultimately I would be immersed in the world of holistic healing and spirituality. I seriously doubted the phrase, 'Trust that God will provide.' Pam seemed to thrive on it. All I could see was what we didn't have and that there was every possibility things were only going to get worse.

I can accept that there are times when God asks us to surrender ourselves to His will. This was one of those times, as far as Pam was concerned. But I kept thinking that we should not expect God to do everything for us. I felt we had to use our talents and gifts to deserve any reward back from the Divine.

Was it actually possible that God could just give us something for nothing? That we could believe in real practical terms what Jesus said: 'Look at the birds in the air, for they do not sow or reap nor gather into barns; yet your heavenly Father feeds them. Are you not of more value than they?' I could see that trust was written all over this, and so like so many times before, I *nearly* surrendered.

CHAPTER 8

Expansion of Consciousness

Pam was a make-it-happen kind of girl. If God said, 'Move to Greystones', there was Pam. If God said, 'Move to Blackrock', then that was where we'd be. Trust was Pam's buzzword, and trust was my biggest challenge. Faith in the existence of God was my biggest gift but along the way I'd lost belief in myself, in other people and life in general. Only a few individuals had gained my trust and Pam definitely deserved that, as well as my admiration. However, she always made a point of asking me to believe in my own divine connection, which I found difficult to do in spite of having had several spiritual experiences. I found it hard to accept what God was asking of me – or even that God would ask me to do anything at all.

I knew I wasn't in charge of my own life any more and that was quite scary. Pam and I debated constantly about the way God works. For me it was: when you use all the talents He gave you, then you give Him the chance of honouring your efforts, and then you deserve to be successful. It would be about plotting a course for the long-term survival of our healing centre so we could help as many people as possible. Pam, on the other hand, was prepared to wait and trust so much more than me as she believed that all progress would be in divine timing. The universe was hell-bent on teaching me trust and patience, and Pam's courage, faith and belief often made me feel guilty, as if somehow it was wrong to give divine providence a helping hand. Pam trusted that abundance would come to us if we just held the space. Honestly, I couldn't decide which was right, so balance became my buzzword.

It was hard not to believe when you saw Pam's faith and trust rewarded, as what she needed was always there when she needed it. Even when she left Achill Pam said she realised that in life you may have to surrender something so God can give you something better in return. Let go and let God. An old Chinese proverb goes, 'Before you fill a cup you must empty the cup first.' So she was always willing to follow where the Divine led. Regardless of how tough things became, she was ready to step back and wait for God's guidance as to what to do next.

Blackrock happened in early 2004. I cannot believe how quickly things changed but God really does move in mysterious ways. The house in Blackrock was ideal. It had a large room on the ground floor that could be used for training and workshops, and a good-sized kitchen which meant that Pam, a fine cook, could prepare meals for trainees. The garage and the attic had been converted into more rooms, and we decided to use the attic as an office. In time the garage would become a crystal showroom. There were four bedrooms upstairs. Two of them remained as bedrooms, the third was converted into a counselling room which doubled as a colour therapy room, and the fourth bedroom became the most important room in the house, the healing room. We were delighted with this room as it was a beautiful space and a perfect place for healings, prayers and meditations and for providing a workspace during our training sessions.

I was aware with each move we made I was surrendering more and more into the work we were meant to do. Invariably for Pam it was all about Spirit, and she believed it was the client's responsibility to find their way to us via divine guidance. This was hard for me because of my sales background. I wanted to reach out and tell the world of a new way of being, a way I believed could really change a person's life. It was a shock to find that there were already many holistic healing and wellness centres open and well established around the country. But each one had their own special qualities, as ours would have too. The twin flame energy could provide its own unique energy and essence, and would attract the clients who were meant to come to us.

The problem was, I was awakening fast but my head or brain could not keep up at times. Now and again I behaved like a little child. Pam had to use all her care, patience and understanding to cope with the reign of chaos which was often created because of my fears, frustrations and doubts. At times I wanted to run and hide, and at other times I wanted to find the stillness, to just accept. But the changes were like a tsunami – you could not hold them back.

Funny how I always thought of God owing us something. Surrender was eventually to be learned and at this time it was a long way off. At this stage I really didn't want to do anything wrong. I wanted to get it right for God and Pam, but didn't feel I could. My own work had diminished but there was still enough money to start moving the healing centre forward. I had been used to being poor before and was never concerned about being wealthy – I was ambitious but it was not about money. I just needed enough to get by. Now I was really trying to commit to this new way of life in the service of Spirit, but I still was afraid that things couldn't and wouldn't work out.

All this time I was working really hard on myself and personal change and growth were constant and sometimes painful companions. My emotions were frequently off-balance as I took my own journey in this touchy-feely world.

So our door in the new centre in Blackrock was now open to clients, and we waited – Pam patiently and me impatiently – for God to send enough people to us so the place could become self-sufficient.

It is interesting the mind of a child! One day I told Pam about my experiences regarding the film, *Darby O'Gill and the Little People*, which I saw when I was a child. I was no more than about eight and my brother Marcus was about five. My sister took us to see the film in the Adelphi cinema in Dun Laoghaire. Sitting in the darkened auditorium and stuffing ourselves with sweets even before the film started was part and parcel of the whole experience. We watched the film and afterwards my sister and Marcus said they really enjoyed it. But I was really frightened by some scenes, and that fear remained in my subconscious until I was forty-five. I was aware of the fear but not the reason for it.

One day in early 2004 when I was with Mum and Marcus in the family home, the film happened to be on the telly and Marcus asked me jokingly if I would like to see it. I said, 'Absolutely no.' I had a definite anxiety about the picture which I knew was irrational. After all, it was a children's film and I was now an adult. When I told the story to Pam she suggested we watch it. We went down to the shopping area of Blackrock and in one of the video stores we saw, guess what? *Darby O'Gill and the Little People* on special offer. So we bought it, and when we went back up to the house we sat down to watch it. I wondered if anything would open up for me so I could understand my fears a little better.

Sean Connery was a young man when he starred in the film, which had wee folk featured in it. The story was that Darby had tricked the king of the leprechauns and taken him captive. The film had some amusing moments in it, and I'm sure for most kids it was very funny. As we arrived towards the end of the film, we learned that Darby's daughter was ill and dying, and a banshee was howling at the window. Then a carriage with a headless horseman came to collect Darby's daughter's spirit and take her home. Darby jumped into the carriage only to see the king of the leprechauns sitting in the corner of the carriage. As he pleaded for his daughter's life, he said, 'Don't take my child! Take me, leave her.'

Of course a sensitive child could see the howling banshee as scary, as well as the carriage coming to take the dead girl. Added to that were the rich colours of the film, the loud music and sound effects in the darkened cinema. But these things were only part of the problem.

It wasn't long before I understood what had happened to me. After I had seen the film all those years ago, I lay in bed that night, frightened of my family being hurt, or of losing them. So I said to God, 'God, if you have to hurt anyone, hurt me. Leave my family alone. Take me.' In that moment I felt I had made a contract with God, a contract that would haunt me deep down till I reached the age of forty-five. After the deaths of two brothers, Johnny and Joey, and the anguish I felt with God for not sticking to His part of the bargain and taking me, I realised that God doesn't work that way. Each person has their own plan and their own life path to follow. I broke the ties with the contract that existed in my child's mind and since then that film no long has any power over me.

It shows how the simplest of thoughts and beliefs can get stuck in a child's mind, and how impressionable children are. Or at least this one was! As I worked through the pain in my inner child, I found many other moments like that which had coloured the beliefs which governed my life. The more darkness I let go of the more the light shone in.

∾

Pam and I had taken a trip to Glastonbury in 2003. While there, I got my aura photo taken by a machine which was a combination of a computer and a camera. I found out later that this machine had a link to Kirlian photography which captures the energy field around the body. One day, while sitting with a cup of tea in the centre in Blackrock, I remembered the machine and wondered how much it would cost. Potentially, we could take it to holistic shows where it could partially finance the healing centre and might also help us get established. Pam liked the idea, and went into investigation mode.

But when she came back to me with the price of the machine, I told her it was too expensive. However, not affected by my reservations, intrepid Pam somehow attracted enough abundance to bring the machine to us. After placing the order, we waited for it with great anticipation. We had planned to take part in the Mind Body Spirit show in Cork that September and we were worried that the machine wouldn't arrive in time. When the box finally arrived, we had to fork out even more money to pay VAT for the item. But once that was done, it was ours!

Pam put the system together and we took pictures of each other to make sure it all worked properly. We were satisfied with the results and by divine providence we were ready, just in time, to brave the show – twin flames ready for action. This was a huge step forward for us as it opened up the possibility of having a lot of one-to-one contact on a regular basis with the public, and it would help us create awareness of the work we were doing.

∽

With the move to Blackrock in early 2004 and with my

foundation level Aura-Soma course beginning in March, things were moving swiftly along. Clients were coming to see us, each with their own story, and Pam and I were learning to work as a team. We were also spending a lot more time together. Pam was a great teacher and friend, and a real support on my awakening to awareness.

In living the way we were, and working in healing, we met many fine people. Geoffrey Healy called over to us one day. He was known for his quality pottery and his spirituality. He had never met us before but to be honest, no one knew us well at that stage. It was shortly after we had been brought together as twin flames. Geoffrey said he'd made a bowl for us. This gift out of the blue from a perfect stranger was surprising, to say the least. I wasn't sure what to say and thought it was just a bit odd. Pam was more appreciative and gracious. I know now that I had difficulty in receiving, as well as not really knowing what he was talking about. I automatically assumed the object was something like a breakfast bowl. Geoffrey said we would have to visit his pottery shop in Kilmacanogue in Wicklow to collect it. We thanked him and said we would call in at some stage.

One day, when Pam and I were suffering from cabin fever, we headed off to Avondale to Parnell's house and gardens in County Wicklow, a place where we would run our first inner child workshops and spiritual weekends. On the way back we passed Geoffrey's shop. We went in and Geoffrey produced the piece of pottery he had made for us. Rather than it being a simple bowl, it was a beautiful centrepiece. We both looked at in amazement. He told us he didn't usually paint his pottery but said he felt guided to on this occasion.

On the bowl Geoffrey had painted a cross in pink and gold, creating four quadrants, with marks in each. You may recall I mentioned in a previous chapter that pink and gold are the colours of our soul bottles in Aura-Soma. Without being aware of it, Geoffrey had created the twin flames' colour combination on the bowl. Then I looked closer at the marks Geoffrey had painted in the quadrants of the cross, and could hardly believe my eyes when I saw they were symbols that represented the four masters Pam and I worked with: St Germain, Lady Nada, Kuthumi and Serapis Bey. These were all confirmations of the link Pam and I had and of the pair of us being twin flames. Geoffrey told us he had also used the Quintessence Serapis Bey in the manufacture of the bowl.

It was a beautiful gift from the hands of a talented artist and a man who was deeply spiritual and divinely guided in the creation of an affirmation of who and what we are.

I always felt Spirit continually supported us through all our upheavals. If it had not been for likes of the bowl, the candle splitting off, and the Aura-Soma bottles, it would have been far easier to give up.

Foundation level Aura-Soma was spread over two weekends. We had just moved to Blackrock and were still settling in when the course started. Cathleen was our teacher and her energy was quite angelic. The first weekend started on Friday. The room was full of people who seemed to have Egyptian past lives, and here I was in the midst of them all. I had already used a fair number of the Aura-Soma bottles and had felt their benefit. I was thrilled to be starting to learn about the system and looked forward to the adventure and knowledge ahead. However, I was not necessarily feeling the same about the clearing that usually happens after these kinds of trainings.

Around this time, when I was working with the aura imaging camera in Dun Laoghaire Shopping Centre, a man came up to me and told me that he worked with people who had Egyptian past lives. Somehow he knew that I had Egyptian past lives, and said that if I needed help to clear blocked energies from that time, to let him know. That was kind of him, but as I always did my healing work with Pam, I turned down his offer.

In a healing Pam gave me around the same period, I got a message that in a life I had in Egypt I was sold into slavery in Egypt, promoted, imprisoned and then rose to prominence. Now, at this course, I would be experiencing yet another level of my Egyptian past life – or lives. As I write this book I don't know at this point if I had more than one life in Egypt. God only knows the full levels of mischief I got up to in the past anyway!

The Aura-Soma course participants were a wonderful group of people and energies were, by and large, harmonious. I did irritate one man. Apparently I had something to do with having his hands chopped off in Egypt in a past life we had shared there. I thought, that's a long time to hold a grudge! After all, you've got two fine and working hands now. As it turned out, it was a weekend where I was to have an expansion of consciousness and a real challenge to my thinking. I was to be introduced in more depth to the elemental kingdom, and was made more aware of the impact my past lives had on me in this life and how they prepared me for service now. I also received more proof of angels, and gained a strong awareness that we know a lot less about ourselves and the world around us than we think.

The teacher talked about how the Aura-Soma bottles consist of qualities from the three kingdoms: the colours of the human and animal kingdom, the essences of the plant kingdom and the vibrational energies of the mineral kingdom. Well, I could understand that anything that exists has a life force, so I could easily accept what was being said. By now I was becoming adept at handling the unusual. I just decided to go with the flow and tried to keep an open mind about everything. I had learned that a blocked mind was a challenge to my angels, and a real chance for them to stir it. So then my highest good was served by being open, which was the path of least resistance.

The next thing we had to do was to pick four bottles, and we would do readings on each other. I was paired with a young woman, and we agreed she would go first. The bottles she picked provoked a sudden fearful response from me. I pulled right back, like you'd see in a vampire film when Dracula recoils upon seeing a cross. I thought this was quite scary, particularly as I was so familiar with the bottles. I never had a spontaneous reaction like this before, but reasoned it had to be about something happening on an energetic level. I pulled myself together as I knew I had to remain calm while doing a reading for the woman. Inside myself, I knew these bottles mirrored something I needed to deal with.

Later, I found it was to do with what I'd got up to in Egypt and once that was identified I cleared and cleansed it from my energy system.

During a meditation the next day I thought it would be a good idea to apologise on a spiritual level to anyone on the course I did anything bad to in Egypt in a past life, and I also cut ties with any of those events that could still cause problems today. The cutting of ties went very well, and I distinctly felt an energy shift in the room, after which the group carried on its learning.

On Saturday evening I was due to see my in-laws who were meeting in Brady's, a busy pub located in Shankill, a suburb on the outskirts of Dublin. I had heard about parking angels and I wanted to check to see if they were real. I sent out the request: If you're really there, I want to park outside the front door of the pub, walk in and have no problem with seating, and get offered a drink as soon as I sit down. Honest to God, as I came to my destination, I saw there was plenty of parking space in front of the pub, and when I went in I saw lots of seats available. When I sat down I was asked straight away by the barman if I wanted a drink. Man, did I want a drink then! Wow, I thought to myself, this happened in Brady's on a Saturday night, a time when pubs would normally be packed. Angels, I believe!

During that night I had really broken sleep. Every time I closed my eyes, I saw two colours, gold and violet, and this combination in Aura-Soma is Bottle Number 39, The Puppeteer, which is associated with Egyptian past lives. By the time morning came around I was stressed and tired. I called Pam on the way to training and she told me to tell the teacher what had happened. At the venue, the teacher walked in and I saw she was wearing gold and violet, the two colours I had been haunted with the night before. Synchronicity gone mad.

In Aura-Soma, the tutors usually wear white, as this does not clash with the wonderfully-coloured bottles. We are the colours we choose and even the colours we wear help to support us in some way. Obviously Cathleen was aware at some level that she needed to wear these colours on this course for what was evolving energetically around her. When I told her about how I kept seeing gold and violet the previous night she said that was interesting. She then added her intuition had told her to start the class that day by sharing some drops from her gold pomander with the group. I knew the angels were at it again.

Then it was my turn to pick a set of bottles. Cathleen came up to me and when she saw my selection said that I'd just finished lifting a curse from ancient Egypt. How did she know I had one? There was no way she could have heard about the experience I had in Achill so this was a definite sign confirming what Pam's Reiki master had told us before, that I would continue to work at releasing the curse from Egypt over the next while, and that it would diminish over time until it was finally lifted. Cathleen's message reaffirmed that I had finally succeeded. I was rattled but happy. Eventually I finished the course, filled with a much greater awareness of the many levels of existence we all lead, the power of Aura-Soma, and about who I was and am.

The following Monday, while doing a healing session at the Blackrock centre, our client, a bright young man, asked me what planet he belonged to. A name came into my head straight away, and I told him the name. After the very full and challenging weekend I had experienced, I just wanted to proceed with a normal session, but then the client asked what tribe he was from on that planet. More information came into my head, and I told him the strange name that came to me, spelling it out for him.

I thought this was pure madness myself. However, Pam was told by Spirit to do a bit of research so she left the healing session and a few moments later came back with her Oxford English Reference Dictionary. She looked up the name I spelled out and there they were: a pre-Christian grouping at the time of Pythagoras. Who'd have believed it? Beam me up, Scotty. That was something I could not have known, but when you are told that Pythagoras was a past life of Kuthumi and the young man I was working with channelled Kuthumi, then all the dots joined up to give me even more awareness and become a more awakened, more conscious being.

Aura-Soma has continued to be a huge part of my life as it adds continuous cleansing and clearing on all levels, and helps to keep my energy fields clear. Some of the bottles I have used down the years have created dramatic change in me, and other bottles have had a much more subtle effect, but all have contributed to who I am today.

When I think of the journey I took from June 2002 to March 2004, a mere twenty-one months, I am amazed. I had gone from being completely spiritually asleep to seeing spirits, talking to dead people, doing Reiki training, working with colour, understanding past lives, awakening to the reality of the elemental kingdom, communicating with angels, dealing with a lot of my own issues and last but not least, getting used to working with my twin flame . . . And hey, I wasn't out of breath yet.

As I lived this new way of life I could see that at times one thing confirmed the next, and the evolving story all linked together. To this day, I sit in awe at our limited understanding of spirits and how they are always around and working with us.

CHAPTER 9

Rollercoaster

By attending our first holistic show in City Hall, Cork, and with the arrival of the aura imaging camera, we had the opportunity to bring the twin flame energy in front of the general public. I felt that was the objective of the exercise: to let people know who we were, and that we were ready to be of service through our therapeutic and spiritual work. It was a very exciting time and I thought I could make a worthwhile contribution. As far as I was concerned, Pam was going to be the star of the show. Her experience was immense and her education in the holistic area showed in everything she did. It was a real privilege to be working together and to see what working with God meant.

Coming from a history of trusting God through thick and thin, I don't think Pam would have been able to work with me if it had not been for divine intervention and the twin flame energy. She was always calm and I was like a herd of elephants on the rampage. A match made in heaven, yes, but sometimes I thought the guys

Upstairs didn't take into consideration my lack of experience and confidence and the fact that I still had little understanding of my gifts. Many times I wanted to run, but didn't, at least not physically. One day I could be really committed and seen to be enjoying doing the work, and the next day be emotionally heartbroken with the path that I was now on.

Pam, too, was excited about attending the Cork show, and was going to give talks as well as work on the camera with me and do aura readings. I felt honoured to be working with her as my Reiki master. I liked the way she spoke and the reverence that she brought to things. I tried to emulate her. Looking back, I know it was all part of my learning process. I was slower at doing aura readings at the show than Pam and when she was off doing her talks I was not able to handle the number of people that came to the stand for readings. In the best interests of those who came to us Pam decided to cancel some of her lectures in an attempt to support me. The aura camera brought in much-needed revenue. It was a good sign and signalled real hope for the future.

It was less than a year since I had completed the Reiki Masters course and I had not yet fully stepped into the mastership. I was surprised that a lot of healers who came to us during the show who were very experienced and had done various different trainings had not encountered subjects such as Atlantean implants and gateway work. But it was great to see people actively listening. All in all, it was wonderful to be able to introduce others to the energy of the twin flames, and the divinity that brought us together as we held the energy of the Christ consciousness in service.

When I look back at the high of the Cork show it was not surprising that I experienced fear afterwards, as it gave me a mirror of the spiritual progress and the depth of spiritual opening I was experiencing. I can see I had tremendously high expectations of what it would be like moving forward. If I didn't get instant success it might give me an excuse to run. This was not the message I wanted to give, but nonetheless things sometimes got the better of me, and my volatility concerned Pam. I was dreadfully insecure, afraid of getting it wrong and screwing up something very important.

Even though we were new to the shows and the camera, we soon developed a following. Many people came to have their auras read and we definitely had a foundation to build on. An idea of doing healing clinics around the country came to me, and would stay with me almost like a dream.

One day back in Blackrock I was told by Spirit to watch a film, *Field of Dreams*. I rented it out and Pam and I watched it that evening. In it there was a clear message: 'Build it and they will come.' Pam was sure God was talking about the healing centre and that success for us would be assured as long as we surrendered. That meant giving up everything so God could give us something better back. I seemed to be blocking the progress by not leaving my family and the community I was part of to fully build what God wanted.

The tug-of-war between a stubborn immovable Gerry and a determined God put Pam in the middle. When we were working well together, it was fantastic, but too often that high was followed by an incredible low. Pam used to call it a rollercoaster. I had a sense of failure of trying to do the impossible. Our client work was sporadic and income small and irregular. My own livelihood was lost now and this was my work, or mission, and I felt I had to focus on making what we were doing viable. Sometimes it seemed that anything that smacked of expansion in a commercial sense was wrong, which was something I just could not understand or get to grips with.

I suppose one of the things I had to give credence to was my need to learn, to grow and to be mentored. I wanted everything yesterday and this put tremendous pressure on both of us. I am sure Pam liked my enthusiasm but would have liked it a bit quieter. Often on a day when I thought of packing it all in, the next day I'd have a brainwave about something that would improve our work, and that would keep me going.

Through all the pain and turmoil Pam was supportive. She held her faith and belief that God was to be trusted and it all would work out in the end. By now it was nearly impossible to get spare time with Jean and the kids. There was always something to talk about with Pam. Many phone calls were made when I came home, and neither Jean nor the kids were happy when they didn't get the time from me they needed and deserved. In some ways I felt I was destroying what God wanted, what Pam wanted, what the world and his cat wanted. Tension and pressures were continuing to rise.

But then there were many times where the heavens would open and give us something amazing that would support the twin flames and convince me that God really did have a plan

105

for us. Pam knew it and did not need convincing. In her eyes we just had to tough it out. Even if we did give up, and considered separating, would we be allowed? I always had more questions than answers and often wished I knew more. It was hard for both of us. Our worlds had been irrevocably changed and only God knew what was going to happen next.

∾

During one of our healing sessions we were shown a previous life where Pam was burnt at the stake, while I was driven away in a cage on a horse and cart. It looked like I had no choice in the matter, but the energy of abandonment Pam felt in that lifetime was very real. It seemed to correlate with this difficult period where I wasn't sure about staying and continuing the spiritual work but there was a real part of me desperate not to recreate this abandonment. That made me more determined to stay because I didn't want to create the same karma for another life. No one was going to be able to say, 'You walked away again.' At the same time, I still wanted to protect my family and this left me in an untenable position.

I was also concerned by Pam's age and health. She was ten years my senior and had gone through a lot of health challenges. While in Blackrock, Pam had two spells in hospital, one a relatively short visit, the other being an operation with recovery time needed afterwards. Her inner strength, courage and determination was absolutely amazing. She never gave into illness and fought to come back to work as soon as she could, even when I encouraged her to take more rest. As I look back now, I acknowledge that maybe my inner being cried out to her to come back to work even if I did tell her to rest.

Just before one of the Mind Body Spirit shows, Pam twisted her ankle. It swelled up like a balloon. We were both stubborn; she said she didn't need to get it seen to, and I threatened her that no X-Ray, no show. She relented and we spent the evening in Cork University Hospital. As we waited three hours for an X-Ray, she kept trying to persuade me to take her away from the hospital. I kept refusing, growing more and more tired of the incessant arguing. Eventually we were told we could go down to the X-Ray department, and so I pushed her there in a wheelchair. Even as I pushed her along, she kept giving out to me, insisting that she would be fine, and to let her go home. When we got to our destination, I saw an old priest sitting there ahead of us. I said to the two of them in exasperation, 'Here, you two talk to one another. I've been given out to all night.' Thankfully, the X-ray results showed she hadn't broken her ankle and by the time we left the hospital Pan was back to her normal warm and friendly self.

A little while later she had to go into hospital again, with a different injury. Sligo General Hospital was the venue on this occasion, and she did manage to escape this time. When we arrived at A & E we were told there would be a considerable wait. There had been a very bad car accident that night and hospital staff were busy dealing with the people who had been injured. We later found out that one of the injured, a young man, tragically lost his life that evening. Under a promise that she'd visit a doctor in Dublin, I got Pam in the car and drove back to Blackrock. She did follow through and got herself checked out a couple of days later. I know I didn't always react in the right way when Pam was sick but it seemed to be, 'You're damned if you do and damned if you don't.' I know if the situations were reversed she'd have made sure I got seen to and looked after.

It would be wrong to give the impression that it was always heavy going; there were as many highs as lows. In between the 'heavies', as Pam used to call them, were tremendous moments of care and support. Most times we worked really well together, with a huge level of mutual respect. We were for the most part able to spend a lot of time talking, debating and enjoying each other's gifts and intellects. If you asked Pam to climb Carrauntoohil, the highest mountain in Ireland, she'd offer to climb Everest. We deeply cared about each other and through the pain there was at times great joy.

Massive abundance was not our thing. We didn't need big cars, worldwide recognition or even popularity. A lot of times we shied away from anything with high visibility. The pressure on both of us was intense and I think we did really well in showing courage and conviction. This was honoured by God as He brought us through horrible obstacles. Vicky Wall, one of the creators of Aura-Soma, used to call it 'the tempering of the steel of who we are'. In essence, what does not kill you makes you stronger. Someone once said, 'May you live in interesting times.' Well, no one could say that we didn't.

Pam needed stillness and peace, and she had given up a lot so we could work together. Her generosity of spirit and her thoughtfulness was amazing. I tried but found it hard at times as I was continuing to work on my own self-development and trying to deal with many conflicted feelings. This often made life difficult. Pam marched through pain and illness, not looking for or needing sympathy. And no matter how tired, pained or difficult things became, I knew she was always in my corner fighting for me.

Pam didn't create the rollercoaster for us both when she came into my life. My life was challenging even then, but also full of magic, joy and happiness. Pam's life and mine were meant to collide through divine planning and timing, not through any intention on our parts. No matter how hard things were at times, this divine planning gave meaning to many of the painful memories and events of my life. It also enabled me to explore my detached self and learn and grow, and in the pain I saw immense fertile fields that had yet to be ploughed.

My thoughts turned to how we could make the best use of the aura camera. I was determined to attend as many shows as possible. At this time a lot of one-day local shows were being held throughout the country, usually on Sundays. Initially it was difficult to gain access to some shows because another person was doing something similar to what we were doing, and the organiser of the shows had a long-standing relationship with them. Eventually, over time, we began to gain recognition for the work we were doing and it wasn't long before we were travelling the country most weekends with the aura camera.

Even though we were getting better known and more clients were coming to us at the Blackrock Centre, finances were always tight and there was never enough money to cover costs. On a bad day it always looked as if progress was too slow and that made it hard to trust.

Our financial highs and lows continued from our first year in Blackrock in 2004 and throughout 2005. Pam's belief kept me going, and God kept her going. I felt as if I was pushing a boulder up a hill and if I heard the word 'trust' once more, I was concerned I might strangle someone. But trust was the one word that made me feel weak and guilty. Admitting failure might have been more financially sensible but we were on a spiritual quest, a mission from God, more important than life itself. Pam was a woman who would not give up. She would endure when I might have run away.

Sometimes I felt like a fighter in the ring. When the chips were down and you were about to be counted out, the lads from outside the ring would come in and hold you up – sometimes so you could be clattered again!

An amusing story that happened around this time involved the quintessence bottles in Aura Soma, which are linked to the ascended masters. Pam always had a well-equipped healing room, a beautifully clear Aura-Soma Colour-Care System set and a full set of pomanders and quintessences. In her healing sessions she used the St Germaine and Lady Nada quintessences and I used the Kuthumi and Serapis Bey quintessences. We both used the Christ quintessence a lot of the time as well. The rest of the bottles stood unopened and unused. As I said, money was tight. One day I arrived in as Pam was heading out to buy an Orion and Angelica bottle from our Aura-Soma teacher. I asked why we could not sell the one on the set and replace it when money came in later. After all, the bottle was unopened, hadn't been used. 'You can't break up the set,' Pam said. Eventually, under the weight of my practical argument, she agreed to sell the bottles on demand from the set, and replace them later. I thought, I can't believe it! I have a victory for business. Pam would have usually trusted God to have the answer, and He did, but just not in the way she expected.

Over the next two weeks one client after another came to us and I was told by Spirit to open various quintessences and pomanders from the set, and use them on whatever client I was working with at the time. Eventually all the bottles were opened. This meant they were going nowhere; they could not be sold. After each session was completed, I would read what that quintessence was for and I found it perfectly matched the client's session and what the client was working on. From then on we found ourselves using all the quintessences and pomanders in the set with the many different clients who came to us. If they needed to continue to apply a certain oil after a session then we would acquire the bottle for them.

I was happy that the oils that both of us were using were now benefitting our clients in the same way they had benefitting me. For years afterwards I had a giggle about how I got the masters to work. However, I'm not sure I look forward to meeting them in person when I cross over. I'm sure, though, that these beings of light have a good sense of humour, or at least I hope so, and doubt they hold grudges but as they say, sometimes you're better off letting sleeping dogs lie, or in this case, masters!

'The lord works in mysterious ways, his wonders to perform.'

CHAPTER 10

Crystals and Radio

The end of the year 2004 showed a marginal income for us; not enough to keep the centre open, but with the camera installed, there was enough to hope that 2005 would be a better year for the twin flames. As it was we had to beg and borrow to keep the place running. There were many parts to creating the centre and there was always room for conflict between Pam and the meaning of spiritual, and me and the meaning of business. We were not a charity, although at one stage we thought of going down that road. We had bills to pay and no working capital. If one of us caught a cold the centre suffered and without cash flow it would have been impossible to keep the doors open. Pam, on the other hand, believed that operating with any idea of commercial intent was anti-spiritual. 'We can't do this', 'We can't do that', 'It's not what God wants.' Friction was inevitable and regular, and we always seemed to be taking two steps forward and one and a half steps back.

I'm sure it was quite wearing for a woman who had lived her faith which had served her well. On the other hand I had spent many years working in the field of sales, marketing and advertising. I reminded Pam one time that the pope had employed a very professional PR and management team when he made a trip to England. I know now part of our journey was indeed to find balance between our two worlds, individually and collectively.

Giving up my own business and handing everything over to our invisible Boss was hard. Losing control and surrendering was something I did not do easily. Even so, the practical part of me saw several possibilities for generating income in this new holistic world. This was not with the intention of becoming rich; it was just so that we could break even and have enough money to live on.

After working with the camera I thought again about setting up healing clinics in a number of locations across Ireland. Initially these clinics would be set up in major locations such as Dublin, Cork, Galway and Limerick. We had found that when people's aura photographs were taken at shows and explained to them, some were awakened to their journeys and asked if they could work through issues with us. But we had only one base in Dublin and that was too far away for many people. I thought that if we established locations around the country this could help people as well as providing the income we needed to support the centre. I even suggested to Pam that I would do all the clinics around the country by myself if necessary. But I just could not get her to agree. She said this was not what God wanted. She said the twin flames were always meant to work together as a team.

I didn't argue any further with her at that time. As far as
Pam was concerned I was too inexperienced to do the clinics
alone. It was yet another challenge for me to be patient. We
did set up locations where people could have their aura photos
taken. They were usually in angel shops and holistic centres
around the country. I still believe we would have integrated
our services better by being able to work with the camera and
do healing sessions as well. It would have improved the income
relative to costs, and if we had done that, the pressure would
have been relieved.

One place we went to was a small angel shop and healing
centre in Skibbereen. Just before we drove down to visit them
for the first time, we discovered that only three people had
signed up for aura pictures. This would not even pay for the
petrol we used on the trip. Pam said we should still go, so
we did, and because of very positive feedback afterwards we
ended up going back there and to many more of these smaller
venues around the country. The figures did build a little. We
also did lots of good work with those we met, and people grew
to trust us. So Pam may have been right, but it did nothing for
my nervous disposition or the bottom line.

It was always hard for me to accept that God had chosen
me to do this type of work and to let go of my fears and be of
service. I couldn't live on trust alone, and felt we had a duty
to do our best and then let God help. Pam and I did try to
compromise, and it was difficult for both of us. It was all part
of the challenge of us both learning and growing together. The
pressure that this created for both of us was enormous.

Each day, week and month we lived hand to mouth. It was

not a nice mix, but a mix guaranteed to help me evolve, and I hoped that one day I might become more like Pam. In the end I had to decide that it was horses for courses: for Pam's journey she had to be true to herself, and for mine I had to be true to myself.

When we went through difficult times, and there was a client to heal, I could put down the debate and go to work, whereas Pam would remain upset for quite a while. It was just how both of us reacted differently to situations. Many a time I asked myself what I was fighting for: any businessman worth his salt would close the door, never to return. They certainly would not have spent their lives chasing what seemed an impossible dream. However, bringing the twin flames together was divine planning at its best, and I would have to really go against God to break with what we were doing.

Because I was constantly stressed with everything that was going on, I frequently had horrible nightmares when I went to bed at night. I would often wake up from them in a cold sweat. In one recurring dream I was blind, naked and lost, walking along busy streets. I felt so exposed, and the dream was so real that when I woke up I feared that I had really become blind. Another dream had me driving my car. Sometimes I could see where I was going but I had absolutely no control over the car. I tried to put my foot on the brake but I couldn't find it. I felt terror as I headed straight for walls ahead of me.

Then there were lots of nights when I couldn't get to sleep at all. I'd lie awake worrying about Jean and the kids. What would become of us all? It was like I was in my own personal hell at times. I spoke sparingly of my concerns to Pam and tried to put a brave face on things as she had enough on her mind as it was. Similarly with Jean. She was going through pain regarding my twin flame situation as well as trying to keep the house running and looking after the kids. In the mornings after bad dreams I tried to function normally. I knew the dreams were not real but the hurt, pain and fear were. But even in this dark night of the soul God was still always there with me. It would be some time, though, before I would learn to completely surrender my life into His hands.

When it came to business decisions, sometimes I would give in and it would later be proved I shouldn't have, and then sometimes Pam would compromise and it would transpire that she should have actually held her ground. She knew it was confusing for me, but as she had already done a lot more inner work than I had, she was always willing to be patient and to give every issue time to unfold the way it was meant to. Pam always wanted us to be equal, but I felt she was the most spiritual, the real healer and therapist, and the most connected to God.

As well as attending holistic shows, we decided to run some shows of our own. We hired venues, and got readers, therapists and retailers on board. Because we needed to carry more stock with us for the shows (signs, display units and tables), we leased a small van. Being a diesel vehicle, it was good value for money. The first show we did was in Dun Laoghaire, South Dublin, followed by one in the Royal Hotel in Bray, County Wicklow. The next one was in Swords and finally we had one in Ballyfermot. Both of these were in suburban Dublin. The shows in Dun Laoghaire and Bray went really well, so we went back and ran two more successful shows there a few months later. However, the shows in Swords and Ballyfermot were not as successful, even though they involved a lot of hard work and time to organise.

Eventually we felt it would be better to let other people organise holistic shows, and we would attend them as exhibitors with the aura camera. The bottom line was, Pam was concerned that organising the shows was pulling us more into the commercial world when our real work was to be in healing and spirituality.

By now we knew quite a few people who ran a number of holistic shows in different locations and we also had access to the Mind Body Spirit festivals in Dublin and Cork twice a year. This was an improvement on the previous year when we had far less ways of earning an income. As well as exhibiting at these shows, we continued to take the aura camera to angel shops and other suitable venues around the country. We also held spiritual workshops and Reiki training weekends and so overall, we were sowing the seeds of what we hoped would secure our centre and deliver on what God wanted.

Pam and I were working very hard to create a good healing centre, but the differences between us often showed. We ended up in a very watered-down version of what I would have liked to do, as Pam felt it would have otherwise been too aggressively commercial for a spiritual centre.

By the time I had accepted that my income was going to come

only from the holistic world, I had totally lost my identity. Nothing mattered more than God's design, and though I had to fight hard to trust it and wait patiently for His plan to be revealed, I really felt I had no choice. The fact that I was still trapped in the two worlds – being married with a family and alongside that fighting for a mission that I was landed into, yet totally believed in – was exhausting, to say the least. I was vulnerable and Pam was concerned that I might walk at any time. This uncertainty did nothing for our stability.

Pam put every penny she could find into the development of the centre. However, I never felt that she understood the amount of financial loss I incurred in the acceptance of the new role I had undertaken. She could see what she was putting in, but not what my involvement in this work had taken out of my pocket. I remember as I let my business go, I was aware I was also letting go of my long-term hopes and aspirations for a successful business, big house and big car. I used to promise myself that one day I would be really financially successful, and now I was saying to myself: for better or worse, this is my new life. I was trying to surrender all I was and everything I had previously dreamed of having.

I came into this reasonably financially secure and by the end of 2005 I was very poor and stressed. In spite of this, with every step we took, Pam hammered home: 'Trust, surrender, God will provide.'

We had a battle royale over getting the van signed. This was one I was determined to win, and we ended up with one of the most psychedelic vehicles you'd ever seen. The sides of the van were full of colour, and the back door advertised the aura camera and the shows we were organising. Pam was embarrassed by it and spent the next while pressing her claim that it did not represent the best of who we were. It never ended until the van was got rid of and was replaced by a car which was nothing but trouble from the start. Even worse, the cars that we had to buy thereafter put so much financial pressure on us that they ultimately destroyed all that we had built up. Now I accept that it was part of the divine plan, but back then it just seemed like a bad decision.

At Christmas, when we still had the van, it was responsible for bringing a group of people into our centre. It had been spotted parked in Blackrock and the lady who saw it brought her whole family into us to have their pictures taken. This gave us enough money to help us over the Christmas period. The van also helped to promote the shows we had organised in Dun Laoghaire, Bray, Ballyfermot and Swords. As a result of the vehicle's successful advertising a good number of people came to us at the shows, and others came to our centre and the angel shops to get their photos taken by the aura camera. We never got the same numbers again after it went.

The new year of 2006 brought struggles for us in January and February, but March was busy. The aura imaging we did nationwide and at the two Mind Body Spirit shows made sure of that. April to August were just about survivable and September and October were busy as we had a big show in both those months. November and December were really quiet. A lot of English card readers came over to do the Dublin show and a thought occurred to me: if they are coming over here, it might be worth it for us to go over there. At the larger shows in Ireland we were able to cover our costs and make a decent profit but it was more erratic with the smaller shows. We were never sure how well a show was going to do. For example, in Navan it could be a good show one month but really quiet the next time we went back. Doing the shows was one of our main areas of income and so we had to take the risk, but it was always a gamble. Dublin was not that large compared with the cities of London, Manchester, Birmingham or Liverpool, and I reasoned that the holistic shows over there would have greater footfall than anywhere in Ireland. Perhaps if we did some of those shows we might resolve our cash flow problems.

The first two shows available to us in England were in Malvern and Aberdeen. The Malvern show was at the end of November and Aberdeen was in early January. Pam and I never did things the easy way and, after working all day, we finished late before leaving for England. After the ferry crossing, it was a long drive to Malvern. Even though the events had been advertised as holistic shows, we were disappointed to see that Malvern was actually more of a Christmas market, and we were doubtful we would get visitors to our stand. But we set up and waited and waited.

We covered the cost of the show but lost money on expenses and petrol. I found it really hard to take, but Pam said, 'Trust'. We drove back home to a bleak Christmas. When we got back to Blackrock I said that after the experience in Malvern, there was no point in doing Aberdeen. Pam agreed to cancel it. It was very strange then that our passes to the Aberdeen show in January arrived in the door even though we had cancelled it. Pam said it was a sign and we should go. I was reluctant.

It wasn't just about the fear of losing money at the Aberdeen show, it was also about the loss of time with family at the beginning of the new year. Eventually I caved in and, frustrated and doubtful, I agreed to go. I just could not see how it could be successful. But you never know with God . . .-

We went via Larne to Stranraer and drove through the night to Aberdeen. I had no idea how far Aberdeen was from the boat and we arrived at the hotel where the show was to be held with a quarter of an hour to set up. We just about broke even again. By now, very tired, we headed home. Pam was in good form, humming, 'Always look on the bright side of life.' If I was to sing a song myself then, it would have been Queen's song, 'I want to break free.' Sometimes positivity could be a pain in the ass. I knew it was not fair for Pam to have to try to keep me up all the time, but it had to be OK to be human, and normal people would be worried by these ongoing financial difficulties. Sorry, Pam, that time I could not see the bright side of life.

On arriving back in Blackrock, there was a message on the answerphone from a woman thanking us for being in Aberdeen, and the massive help I had given her at the show. Pam said, 'See, I told you we were meant to be there.' I think I just smiled sweetly. For the moment, adventures to England were to pause and we were to concentrate on Ireland. It was safer and cost less.

∽

While working with the aura camera in a Mind Body Spirit

show at the RDS in Dublin (the Royal Dublin Society is a large venue which holds many exhibitions and events), we tried to improve a return on our stand by selling a small collection we had of crystals, oils and spiritual books. We also thought of starting up a little online catalogue to help the centre. Unfortunately, the catalogue never happened, but somewhere along the way we attracted the attention of crystal people from England.

Always looking to build on a support structure so we could keep our doors open, I chatted about crystals to two very nice people, Roger and Jane, at that particular show. It was suggested we might have mutual interests in selling their crystals in Ireland. We all sat down and discussed their proposition, which involved us acting as an agency and getting commission on the crystals we sold for them. It seemed like a good deal, but we weren't to know then that the couple's business in England was floundering.

A stunning range of crystals could really boost our income, or so we thought. Roger and Jane subsequently came to the Blackrock centre and turned the converted garage into a beautiful crystal showroom, and we started our journey through crystals. From then on, it was decided that Pam would work on the camera at the shows and I would do the crystals. It meant the costs would be shared and the turnover would be doubled.

Maintaining supply of the crystals and working on commission was not easy, as payment was slow. At first we paid over all the money we got to Roger and Jane, and they paid the commission back to us. This was an arrangement, based on trust, we had all agreed to. But as payment as well as flow of products to us got slower and slower, we decided to take the commission out of the money we took in, and then return the rest to the irritated but accepting couple.

The Crystal Bible was the name of a book popular with many of our customers. Despite repeated requests to Roger and Jane for the book, and repeated promises from them that they would send it to us, no books came. Finally, they told us they couldn't get it because it was out of print. As it happened, we had arranged to do another show in the UK, in White City in London, around that time. Pam and I decided to visit a crystal wholesaler while we were there to check on the availability of stock. By now, Roger and Jane were not keeping us well supplied with crystals at all.

When we went to the wholesaler, lo and behold we found out that *The Crystal Bible* was in fact not out of print! We bought two boxes of the book and headed to the show in White City. Again, we just about broke even. Another disaster. Our plans of doing more shows in England now ended, and we decided to rely solely on the Irish market.

On returning home, Pam said we should buy the crystals ourselves. I wasn't so sure; we'd have to invest in stock and again money was tight. I wanted to give Roger and Jane another chance. Pam said I was being codependent. In the end we went with Pam's plan, loaded Roger and Jane's crystals, stands and paperwork in the car and set off for England. We returned everything back to the couple, and on the way home purchased our own range of crystals, which we sourced ourselves.

This was to become a regular trip. I sold some of the crystals

I got in the UK to retail customers we had in Ireland and this paid for the trips and repaid the costs of our bulk orders, whilst leaving enough crystals for our own stands. This method of business minimised the negative effects on our cash flow. This system worked well as we continued to develop a good range of crystals to display at shows and at the Blackrock centre.

As 2006 progressed, it started to look like we were developing well. 2005 sales had dipped when compared with the year before but we just had to accept that life was full of ups and downs. We were always trying to make it work, and no one could fault our efforts.

∾

One of the interesting sideshows in 2006 was as a result of working with the aura camera in Dun Laoghaire Shopping Centre. A young woman came up to our stand and asked if we'd like to go on the radio. She presented her own show from a local Dublin radio station, Anna Livia. We both thought it would be a good idea, and went up to her home to set up the interview and discuss the topics we would talk about. On the morning of the show, both Pam and I went to the Anna Livia studio. Our presenter flew in the door very close to our starting time, with a breezy comment of forgetting her notes.

'Not to worry,' she said, 'We'll just wing it.'

It certainly knocked us off balance. What we had prepared was thrown out of the window. We had no idea of what was going to be said or asked, and we had friends and family listening in. Thankfully, the interview went well, and we covered most of the information that had been on the brief. There was also an unexpected bonus. I had always been quite shy and was afraid of speaking in public, never mind the radio, but with Pam's support, this baptism by fire to the world of broadcasting left me completely cured of my fear.

Next, we found ourselves discussing doing a show that would run for twelve weeks. Each show would be one hour in length. We hoped it would be an opportunity for us to get the Blackrock centre recognised in Dublin. Two days before the show was to air, we heard our presenter had been taken ill. We went to Anna Livia and told them our situation. They said fine, but added that we had to follow up on our agreement to do the twelve shows. We had to accept that we had to do all the production and broadcasting ourselves. So the twin flames successfully aired the first show together, and then kept it going for the following eleven weeks. I don't know if we gained anything out of the shows, but the experience of being on air was an example of how we could adapt to just about anything that was thrown our way.

I know that God thinks very differently about the world than we do. He always gave Pam and I just enough to do what was needed, but never enough to be comfortable. We had loads of experiences of the Divine in our lives, which helped us function, but we never did well enough to provide any form of security for ourselves. Each year something new would be introduced to build on the year before, but then what worked in the previous year would not work the following year.

My work in the healing room left no doubt that I was spiritual and gifted, but I worried that it was taking a long time for us to become established. In a way I felt like the Hebrews wandering in the desert, who seem to have had the worst tour guide in history. It took forty years for them to go from one place to the next! I was also concerned that it was me who was holding us back, because I kept wanting to use my own free will instead of surrendering to divine will.

Through all the turmoil, we continued to work on each other to clear our respective issues from the past. Because of this, our spiritual gifts opened up more, as well as our stamina. Every emotion you could care to mention we brought up in one other, which was painful at times, but we persisted because we believed one hundred per cent that was what God wanted us to do.

It was at times a most amazing, if very wearing, journey for both of us.

CHAPTER 11

The Masters Cometh

Who is God? Who are Archangel Michael, Archangel Gabriel and all the other angels and masters and saints? And what do they look like? None of us really knows. Over millennia our heritage, our teaching and our traditions have combined to create different impressions of God, the angels and other heavenly beings. However, the paintings and sculptures we have seen of our Creator and other spiritual beings are not factual pictures of same. As we evolve, we can accept that God chooses the form He comes to us in, and that can be different for everyone. At the end of the day, it is our faith and our trust that are pathways to God.

We won't discover answers by trying to scientifically prove whether or not God exists. Science can only provide questions and theories, not answers, and scientific truths are movable as we learn, discover and understand more. I am not anti-science; it's more a realisation that the more we know the more we don't know.

So when I say I communicate with God, ascended masters, angels and spirits and have some understanding of past lives, there is no way for me to prove I am telling the truth. All I can do is ask you to accept that I have experienced these things. For example, how do I know that Christ was in our healing room? He certainly didn't provide me with a photo ID. I know it because I felt it and because of His promise, 'Where two or three are gathered in My name I am there also.' I know where I am coming from and those working with me do too. I believe that God has revealed a part of Himself to me and He also does to anyone who is spiritually open. We can all see God's work in the miraculous beauty of nature – in a beautiful sunrise, a cascading waterfall, or the mesmerising murmuration of starlings when they swirl across the sky in beautiful shapes. But none of us can actually know the fulness of God.-

Theologians may contest the veracity of what I've written. They might quote scripture to prove that I am wrong, but from the time I was told by my mother of the wise men following a star to Bethlehem, I believed in signs, and when I read of the shepherds hearing heavenly music and the angels telling them where the holy family was, I believed in angels, and from the moment I heard about Jesus, a carpenter who called fishermen, a tax collector and other ordinary people to follow him, I believed that God cared for all of us equally. When I read the story of the Holy Spirit Who descended over the disciples as flames of fire and gave them the strength to go out and preach and heal in the name of Christ, I believed in God's absolute love and care for his people.

People say bad things happen on Earth, and they do. But we

can only look at part of the picture. We cannot know the mind of God, and so our judgements can be premature.

We may think that we are innocent of the world we create, but with free will we make choices every day that affect our world and our planet, and we disempower ourselves when we put the blame on God's shoulders. It is only when we choose to care for our world that we see how much of a difference we can really make.

So who is to say that God can't talk to or work with ordinary people like myself? I am as surprised as anyone that He chose me to be of service to him in this lifetime. I wouldn't put myself down as God's first choice! But again, we can't know or determine how the heavens operate, because that would be ego (Edging God Out) beyond belief. What will bring us closer to God is a willingness to be kind, understanding, compassionate and respectful to everyone and everything.

I always base my belief in God on love. Through the healings that clients have received from God through Pam and me, I've seen many people let go of pain and hurt. Is it my gift to them? No, not a chance. The healings come from Christ, the angels and other heavenly beings. I am but a pair of hands, a simple overweight balding man that God has irritated and agitated to do this work for Him. Like a solicitor, doctor, teacher, farmer or road sweeper, we all have a sacred mission and should value our work. God's children are a team and no head should be higher or lower than anyone else's.

If you want to see miracles in this book, see them in the simplicity of service, the support that we shared with others on this mystical journey, and the beauty of the people God sent our way.

I have no doubt that Christ brought Pam and myself together as twin flames. I also have no doubt that despite all the pain that we have suffered since, He and the world of Spirit have been ever-present in our lives and will continue to be till we both pass. My door to the spiritual world has opened and I cannot close it again.

When I hear people say, 'I've found God', I always feel a little left out. Nobody tells me anything. I never heard He was lost. No matter the darkness of the times we go through, His light is always shining the way. Sometimes, to us, He is in the background and sometimes he is carrying us. But He is never separate from us, and not just the privileged few, but all of us, every moment of our lives. 'I hold you in the palm of My hand,' He says, and I believe He does.

I do not do miracles, or make people walk or stop people dying. I don't do anything, but God can do all at any moment. Sometimes the miracle is a walk through the door of death with hope, not fear. Sometimes it is acceptance of something. Sometimes it is the knowledge that you never ever walk alone, and all you have to do is ask for healing, or for help. He may not fix you the way you want to be fixed, but He will give you strength, courage and peace. He will give you what you need even if this is not what you want.

∽

The next few stories are to show you how strong and personal our journey was.

Christ is always in the healing room but He has really made

130

His presence felt on a small number of occasions. During one of those times I could feel His energy step into my body. I'd go all goosepimply, then hold my breath. The stillness was amazing. But I never felt He was there for me. I knew He was there for the person on the plinth. As Pam and I worked away on the client, the room would be filled with a gentle sacredness. When the session was over, and Christ had done what He wanted to do, He stepped back and left space for us to get on with the work He wanted us to do in His name.

Frequently during a session a client would feel a hand working on a part of their body where we were not working. We'd just grin and say it was normal. But in spite of these amazing incidents, I sometimes still felt like an errant child; I would not surrender fully, and I would not trust fully. I was far removed from being holy – I was even given out to at times by Archangel Michael! I often thought I was not good enough for God to bother with.

Somehow, though, I never felt frightened, never felt in awe, I just thought it was all mad, but I had to sort of accept the madness. Pam would feel slightly irritated by my language sometimes. 'Freaky',' Scary', 'Weird', were not words that she used to describe sacred events. She would sometimes have thought I was disrespectful to what was going on. I wasn't – I just didn't know how to react to these incidents.

Then we had the antics with the aura camera. Initially, when we got the camera, we needed a lamp to shine on a curtain we used as a backdrop so we could see a person's aura properly. After a while things changed. We noticed that the bio sensor box often picked up energy fields around the room and projected them onto the curtained backdrop. The moving energies could be seen very clearly. At times the energies were hazy, other times coloured, and sometimes they had discernible physical features. We learned that there were different types of energies. Spirits used to say hello, angels and masters used to visit and I was also at times asked by other spirits to do gateway work. I wasn't always happy with this, but it was all about learning and growth. Eventually we got used to it, and it was a sure way of spirits getting our attention. Ultimately we didn't need the lamp any more, as the spirits provided all the light we needed. They always hovered around the seat our clients sat on, and the light of their spirit energies helped us see clients' auras much more easily.

Remember Malvern? Well, when we set up the camera there, we saw spirit energies on the camera and got a message from Spirit that they were a group of Saxon soldiers from the Battle of Hastings who were waiting to wake from their sleep and go Home. I said the prayer for them to find peace and they crossed over into the Light. As we left to return to Ireland, I was tired and stressed because I'd had a long week. We arrived back in Dublin and Pam continued travelling on down to Kilkenny as she and a friend were scheduled to work at a show there. I had planned to get through some work in Dublin. Kilkenny had been advertised as a holistic fair, but it turned out to be another Malvern. At about eleven o'clock in the morning Pam rang me.

'You have to get down here now. I've got spirits on the camera who want to go Home.'

'I can't, I'm busy here,' I said. 'You can do the prayers yourself.'

However, Pam was still not happy, so in the knowledge that my time doing commercial work was disrupted yet again, I grudgingly headed off to Kilkenny.

We accept that air is all around us, even if we can't see it. Well, Spirit is all around us all the time, whether we are aware of them or not. The aura camera picks up the very essence of Spirit, so it was no surprise that the sensors picked up these spiritual beings. When I arrived at the show, Pam told me she had counted thirty-three faces going across the screen of the imaging machine. When I looked at it I could see she was right. You could see them clearly. I did a little research and found that the area in Kilkenny we were in was built on a village that had been sacked during Cromwell's invasion in the 1600s, and thirty-three would not have been far off the number of those who had died there. I sat down, lit a candle and did the prayers. Holding the space, I called in Christ to be with me while I did the work. I cleared thirty-one of them and then I discovered that the last remaining two of this earthbound group were Cromwellian soldiers who had perished at the village as well.

'No,' I told Pam, 'I can't do this. Not after what Cromwell did to my country. No, I can't.'

I was metaphorically stamping my feet like a bold little boy.

'No, not Cromwell's men,' I said again.

Pam pointed out that God decides who we are of service to, not us.

'But look what Cromwell's soldiers did,' I protested.

I didn't see how irrational it was that I sent English soldiers Home the previous week in the UK, and now was refusing point blank to help two of Cromwell's men cross over. It never ceases to amaze me how our subconscious can control our lives and what lurks in the shadows of our being. Here I was refusing to send spirits Home because of some deep-rooted feeling of national injustice, a nationalism which was part of my conditioning through my family line and history.

Well, after about half an hour I relented and helped these two men to cross peacefully. I suppose it was a lesson for all of us as to how prejudice and hurt of the past can control us a lot of the time, without us even being aware of where it comes from. If we look at it another way, Cromwell's men were wanting to teach me about deep-seated beliefs that I needed to clear to be able to grow spiritually. Thanks, Cromwell's men.

The house in Blackrock was lovely and peaceful. A few weeks after we started doing therapy work and healings, a group of young men working for a telephone company started to drill outside the wall of the garden. Apart from slightly disturbing the ambience of the place, the noise didn't bother us too much. However, we soon realised that the disturbance of the earth had awakened energy lines around and in the house, and as a result the house had become very spiritually active.

One day, after being out and about for a while, I arrived back at the house to see poor Pam sitting on a chair halfway down the garden.

'I'm not going back in there till you send those spirits Home,' she told me.

I laughed, went into the house, said the gateway prayers and cleared the house of the spirits present at the time. It became something I had to do quite often there as spirits became aware it was an exit point from where they could be sent Home.

At the Mind Body Spirit shows in the RDS, Dublin and also at some of the other holistic shows, one of my spirit friends, Ascended Master Kuthumi, often appeared on the aura camera. He seems to have a sense of humour. On that particular day Pam, who was always very precise in lining up the camera, had a client sitting in the chair. As she was about to take the picture Kuthumi peered out at the camera from behind the client on the right. Pam was not amused and reset the camera. Kuthumi then did the same on the other side of the person. After this happened a third time, she said to me with great exasperation, 'This is your fella. Sort him out.'

'Yeah right,' I said. 'As if he's going to do what *I* tell him.'

Anyway, it seemed Kuthumi was finished with his little joke, because he behaved for the rest of the day. He continued to visit us every now and again. Whenever we saw strong gold behind a person we knew it was your man.

The aura camera once gifted us with a truly amazing phenomenon. One day, at our Blackrock centre, Pam set up the camera for a client who was coming to get their aura picture taken. She went back downstairs to prepare breakfast and I walked into the room to collect an Aura-Soma bottle. Suddenly I noticed a stunningly bright and glowing white spirit on the computer screen.

'Who are you?' I asked in wonder.

'Christ,' the Spirit replied.

I shouted down the stairs to Pam, 'Hey, Jesus is here!'

Pam came up the stairs to see me trying to send Christ Home.

'What are you doing?' she said.

I told her I was sending the spirit Home.

'You can't do that,' she exclaimed.

'Of course I can,' I retorted. 'I'm checking to see he is who he says he is. If He is our Boss He won't go Home, and if he isn't I will just have sent an earthbound spirit Home.'

I suppose in my heart I knew it was not an ordinary spirit, as Pam and I had got used to seeing spirits of the higher realms on the camera. They were always brighter, stronger and much clearer than spirits who had lived an ordinary human existence.

When I'd finished my vain attempts at sending Him packing, I heard Him clearly say that He was making his presence felt because He knew we needed his support on a deeper level for one particular client who was coming to us for healing later that day. He also promised that we would have a visit from Him and four of the ascended masters we regularly worked with at a Mind Body Spirit show that was coming up soon. God is determined to wreck my head, I thought. What would we say to people if they saw ascended masters walking down the aisles of the RDS? How could we begin to explain the unexplainable?

Even though we knew Christ was ever-present in the healing room, we had never actually seen His energy spirit until now on the camera. We had always been aware that during healings He held the space and supported us. That day, after each client's session finished, we checked on the computer screen to see if Elvis had left the building. It was only after the very last session that He disappeared from the camera. Over the years I began to accept that this event was a once-off, only to be surprised recently when He did it again. I am still learning to accept that Spirits do not work according to our rules or agendas, and do things in their own way and in their own time.

The Mind Body Spirit show started inauspiciously. We always wanted to get the best value for money and tried to choose a stand where we would have high visibility. Our stand that day was supposed to be a corner unit, open on two sides, but when we arrived we found we were boxed in by another stand, and had only one small opening. After complaining to the organisers, which we rarely did, they moved us. Because of the move we ended up with a stand three times the size of the one we originally ordered for the same money. We had little to fill it with but did our best with what we had. When the show opened, we sat awaiting our spirit visitors.

When the camera was turned on, the first spirit appeared on the screen. It was slightly duller white than Christ's Spirit which had appeared on the camera in Blackrock, so we knew this to be Serapis Bey, one of the masters I worked with during healings. Then a while later a gold stripe joined the white of Serapis Bey. This represented Kuthumi, another of the masters I work with. After the same length of time a pink stripe appeared: Lady Nada. Next came a violet stripe, which was the calling card of St Germaine, and finally a red stripe, which in this instance signified the presence of Christ. I was so grateful that all the spirits' presences were with us, and that they were well behaved for the entire show. I was also relieved that they were not there in physical bodies!

All these spirits appeared over the three-day period of the show, each one joining in the exact length of time between them, so that each of the masters were recognised individually. A few clients who came to us for aura pictures were aware of ascended masters and were fascinated when we indicated to them what was happening. The full display of hues was completed a few hours before the show ended, and it was a beautiful blend of gold, pink, violet and red against the white of Serapis Bey.

Every time we did a show Pam insisted on dedicating the stand to the service of God, and that people would leave the stand with whatever healing they needed, whether they bought something or not. We were there for other people, not for ourselves. Every time something special like the masters appearing happened, it left us in no doubt that what we did mattered, and that Pam and I were in sacred service. We were prepared to give God what He wanted, regardless of whatever anxieties we might have had.

∾

Down the years I have heard of attacks on healers and the work they try to do by various religious and spiritual organisations. This is sad. Also, recent scandals in churches of all denominations have shaken people to the core. Unfortunately, in every organisation there are some who misuse or misrepresent what they are doing. Why, in my mind, do we place our spiritual well-being in the hands of other people? How we connect with God or Spirit is for us to decide.

There are great people in religions of all denominations. There are also great people in the area of healing who really care for the clients who come to them. It is crucially important that the world holds its spirituality. If it doesn't we will hand over a more fearful life to our children.

It is my fervent hope that we all start to see the good in people of every belief and persuasion. The only time we will know full spiritual truths is when we pass into spirit and I believe it will be a Home for all, because God loves all of us equally.

When we look in the shadowy darkness of life all we can sometimes see is the darkness – but look for light and you will see it is there. Many people dedicate their lives to help, serve and protect others, and often put themselves in harm's way to be there for people in need. There is no doubt that Pam and I struggled with tremendous darkness. We also experienced many blessings along the way. Meditation, prayer, trust and surrender one day at a time helped us weather many storms. We also had many laughs. God is light and love and to this day I don't see the journey as a punishment, but as a gift.

It is up to us to shine our light and help others to shine theirs.

CHAPTER 12

A Practical Move

By now the pressure was really starting to get to us financially. Pam was still saying, 'Trust', 'Believe', but we kept having to run faster to stand still. Each year we would try new innovations but as soon as we'd do or get one thing right, another thing would go wrong. I'm sure we could have been forgiven for thinking that God was against us. But we really did believe He was supporting us, although at times I was confused. Pam remained resolute in her absolute belief that in the end God's plan would reveal itself and everything would happen in divine timing.

I was always pushed off balance by the instability of our income. Despite our best efforts this meant that by the end of 2006 I felt we'd have to give up. The only other option was to reduce costs and find a way of increasing sales. At that time we were renting the house in Blackrock and Pam also had her place in Achill. There was broad agreement that the combined rents were too high.

Currently, Pam's old house was rented by us as a retreat centre. I was aware early on that this would not work. There were not enough people willing to travel to Achill, and it was a white elephant. I wanted desperately to pull out of this situation as we didn't have the cash flow to support it. As it turned out we eventually had to borrow again to pay off that debt.

As well as that, having to stay in hotels as we travelled around the country added a crippling cost to our already straitened finances. So at the end of the day we agreed to give up both Blackrock and Achill and rent a more affordable and convenient place that would be the new venue for our centre. We found a house in Longford that suited these needs. The rent was lower and it was a good mid-way location in relation to going back and forth to shows around the country. It also meant far fewer overnight stays in hotels.

Moving out of Dublin and giving up Achill was hard on Pam, but she did everything to make things work. However, I didn't realise how unhappy she was going to be in Longford. She had thought I was going to move there with her, but I still wanted and needed the connection with Jean and my children and decided to stay based in Dublin. When Pam discovered I was not going to join her, she was not a happy bunny. I should have been more sensitive to her needs but in this matter, I thought logic won the day – or at least I convinced myself that this was the case. The reduction in costs would take a massive amount of pressure off our shoulders and this would calm the situation down considerably.

I was still hanging tough and trying to do God's work on

my own terms. But I was hurting Pam by leaving her alone in Longford, and also hurting my family in Dublin because I was not there enough for them. It always seemed as if we were battling against the tide and things were always going askew. I continued to have my 'out of control' dreams, and they became more frequent and intense. My stress levels were increasing and suicidal thoughts were beginning to creep into my head. I felt very alone, and kept beating myself up with conflicting thoughts. Why couldn't I just do what God and Pam wanted and needed? But then, why wasn't it right for me to do what *I* wanted?

Spirit kept supporting me as I continued to learn and develop spiritually, but in spite of that, I began to feel worse and worse and more anxious about the future. I had tried everything I knew to help Pam and myself earn a living, but so many things were going wrong. I also worried that if I gave up working with Pam it would mean I was giving up on the healing world, and going against God. And what would happen if I took control of my own future again and turn my back on what God wanted? I was torn apart as I tried to find a solution to my problems.

In the midst of all this, Christ was always with us in the work we were doing, but it was like He was separate, serene and detached from all the turmoil I was going through.

∽

It was after a show in Limerick when we finally agreed to change the van. We went to a mechanic in Mayo Pam often used and bought a second-hand car from his garage to replace the van. Pam then traded in her own car for a nearly new one. But my 'new' second-hand car kept having problems. It broke down and had to be towed to the garage twice in as many months. It was amazing how every time I wanted to have quality time with my family the car let me down.

'This never happens,' the mechanic said as he looked at the car. 'It just doesn't happen.'

The car seemed to be cursed with unique problems. However, Pam believed one hundred per cent in our mechanic and car supplier. She loved the make of car, even though I had huge reservations about it. These doubts came from the fact that my dad and brother were both mechanics and I knew they did not have faith in this brand of car.

After spending time being chauffeured around on the back of a pickup truck, my car, Bluey – as the car was affectionately known – had to be changed. By now the costs of keeping our cars on the road were mounting. I was worried but Pam just kept trusting. Our monthly payments were manageable but I was on a cost-cutting crusade. I also had to be realistic. Moving the centre to Longford meant that we were leaning on the cars quite a bit, so they had to be roadworthy.

It wasn't long before we were back with our friendly mechanic, trying once again to solve the problems of the cars. Now a beautiful black goddess, with only 27,000 km on the clock, awaited us. Pam loved it. It was a comfortable estate car, with leather seats that supported her back. It also had plenty of room for carrying everything to the shows. I was very pleased as well, as now we could drive in peace and style and comfort when we were going around the country. I also got a low-cost runaround to try and keep car repayments in check.

You're not going to believe this. The beautiful black estate broke down on the first day. It had to be lift towed and we had to get a rental car to go to the Cork show. When I talked to the mechanic, I told him I had noticed soot all over the turbo and around the engine which I thought shouldn't have been there for a car with such low mileage.

'Nothing to worry about,' the mechanic assured us. 'That's quite normal for those cars.'

A few days later, as we were driving, a warning light came up on the dashboard. My father always told me that whenever this light appears, you need to get your car seen to straight away. So back we went to the mechanic. He said the light was only a computer glitch. Pam believed him, and I felt I should as well. So, reluctantly, I decided to trust the mechanic and keep the car on the road instead of listening to my intuition and to what my father and brother had told me about that make of car.

We had taken out a small loan to help develop the healing centre, and as we now had moved to Longford, the savings on the rent alone more than compensated for this relatively small investment. Actually, this investment helped our turnover to grow to four times what we were earning in Blackrock, and was well in line with practical norms. In truth, we seemed to be making good decisions, bringing income and expenditure into a far better balance.

With all the disasters that were going on around us, it was easy to forget that there was always growth and development happening as well. We had started with nothing, and in the space of a few short years, we had established a strong healing clinic in Dublin, and had run a range of workshops. Along with this, we had earned a reputation for doing aura readings around the country, and also had a good range of crystals which we brought with us to all the shows. We were constantly expanding and innovating and there was a high degree of co-operation between Pam and me in many different areas of the work we were doing.

The next thing we needed to do was promote ourselves. I hoped to greatly strengthen our marketing base to bring more of the public to our doors. Despite previous misgivings about marketing and promoting the healing centre, Pam now seemed to understand the spiritual good this could do. We had high hopes of where we could go. I don't think Pam was ever really comfortable with marketing and sales talk, but as we reached out to more and more people we both saw things could work if we could find a balance between a gentler kind of marketing and a more practical spirituality.

What kept me going throughout the whole journey was the work we were doing with our clients. It was rare that a day would go by without a gift from Spirit. The healing room was a sacred place where we had the privilege of meeting the true spirit of the clients. It was also where we saw the light in people emerge and grow out of the trauma in their lives. We saw individuals with tremendous courage facing some of the worst moments in their lives. Often I had people come off the plinth in floods of tears after opening up some of the pain that had kept them trapped in the shadows. From these healing releases they were finally free to change their lives and create a new future for themselves. As long as these people were coming to us, we could carry all the other challenges. I carry hundreds of their stories in my heart which I will never write in a book, because the client's journey has to remain confidential.

Around this time Pam and I decided to make a meditation CD. I also helped to create the music for the meditation with a mutual friend of Pam's. This was the first time in my life I actually prepared a script for anything, and I was pretty happy with what I'd done. Pam and I had written our scripts separately and didn't know what material the other had.

At this point I was driving the little runaround old car that was part of the deal when we acquired the black goddess estate car. On the day we went to the recording studio in Kildare, which happened to be my birthday, I noticed that my car was making a funny noise. I was worried but decided to put my concerns on hold until after the recording. We went in and set up everything. Pam recorded her piece first, and to my dismay I realised that her meditation included a lot of the exact same imagery as mine. When it was my turn to record I knew I couldn't use my own script and had to wing it instead. To my surprise I was able to and it worked out just fine. It goes to show that when plans don't work out, sometimes it's to pave the way for something better to happen.

The rest of that day was to be spent with my children, but guess what, when I got back in the car after the recording, the noise was still there. Sorry, kids, day cancelled. I knew the car had to get back to the garage quickly. Off I headed up to our sainted mechanic in Castlebar, but a pulley wheel broke off the engine block in Longford and the car ground to a halt. Luckily it stopped almost outside where our healing centre was, and I was able to wait there for the lift tow to come and bring the car to Mayo.

When the car got to the garage in Castlebar the mechanic called me up and uttered the phrase that was becoming all too familiar.

'This does not happen to our cars.'

Yet now this car, the same make as Bluey, shared its disease. The cost of fixing the car and paying for the lift tow made it easier and cheaper to buy yet another car, a Ford Focus, instead. Finally, I had a car that didn't cause problems.

It was near Christmas, and in my Christmas stocking Pam placed a toy Model T Ford car. This came about because when I was doing the aura readings, I used to say to people who were perfectionists that Mr Ford would never have made the Model T if he had seen the Focus. We can sometimes block our efforts to create something good if we don't accept anything except pure perfection from the word go. This can stop us learning for fear of making mistakes. Sometimes we need to accept what we do is good enough, perfect enough at the moment, and then if we want we can rework and improve our creation over time to produce better and better 'models' of that project, passion or endeavour.

∽

Another cost-saving plan we had was simple. We leased a photocopier from a reputable company to print covers in full colour for the aura reports we gave people after they got their aura photos taken, and it so happened we also received an A4 Risograph printer for free from a friend of mine at the same time. The Risograph was a cross between a photocopier and a printer, and was able to run large quantities of pages cheaply in black, red, green and blue ink. We also bought an A3 Risograph to produce a magazine in-house to promote all that our centre was doing, and to print advertising material at low cost for the shows. All this was to improve communications with our clients and the general public.

This enterprise reduced our printing costs and enabled us to save money on our brochures, advertising and teaching notes. We also planned to produce and sell booklets that gave information on and awareness of our inner child and codependency workshops, as well as spiritual weekends. Pam was to write the content of the booklets, as I wasn't qualified to write about these subjects at that point. However, the booklets never happened because there was never enough time for Pam to sit down and write them. This meant the machines that should have been self-financing and potentially profitable never produced what they could have done, but they still gave us the ability to promote ourselves which did bring in a lot of work down the years.

It was only when the photocopier's free ink ran out, courtesy of the sales executive, that we found his calculations were off. The price of producing the covers had turned out to be more expensive than we were led to believe at the time. That was disappointing, but we were still determined we could make it work. At least the Risograph afforded us many options, and worked very well in producing all our printing needs in-house.

I felt increasing pressure to surrender and permanently move to Longford. I even got lectured by two close friends of Pam who felt I should just give up and cast my family aside for God's mission. They told me it wasn't fair to Pam. On about four occasions, as I was driving from Dublin to Longford, I parked up beside one of the lakes, just outside Mullingar.

I was beginning to understand what true despair was, and debated the merits of death over life. I really thought there was no victory in any of this for me. Often I sat by the lake, tears running down my face, and watched the calm and peaceful waters inviting me in. I just wanted it all to end. I thought that if I went then it would all be over. Pam could get on with the healing centre and I would protect Jean from all the hurt and pain of me separating from her. I know that doesn't make sense but it did at the time.

I felt very alone as I begged God for mercy. How could I make this work? I loved my family. How could I leave my wife? How could I do that to her? Furthermore, my mum, whom I dearly loved, would be heartbroken if I broke up my marriage. I was really ready to just go Home; it would have been easier than what was asked of me. But I loved God and could not deny at this stage the truth of what He wanted to create with Pam and me: God wanted the healing centre and wanted me to surrender. However, in my heart I still could not do it.

Because of how I felt then, I now understand how people can

be in so much despair that death seems the only answer. It really helped teach me to understand suicide without judgement.

Somehow He brought me back from the brink during these times of great distress, but He sure did not make things easy along the way. My mother-in-law used to say, 'Don't let anyone grind you down' and my mother's version of that was, 'It's not how you go down that matters, it's how you come back up.' These two inspirational women had a profound effect on my ability to never give in, but it really was desperately hard to persevere during those times.

Maybe Pam thought my practical head took no cognisance of her pain or hurt. This was not totally true; I did see it. I experienced the same pain, but could not give it any space. I had to get on with it and keep fighting but I had very little left to give. I tried to understand more, to believe that everything was to be done in God's divine timing. The thought of surrendering kept following me, but I kept resisting. I accept that I have a real stubborn streak, and it was the love of my family that often kept me going. I thought things might settle and life would become a little easier in time, and some of our better decisions seemed to give us a chance of this happening.

The healings continued and so did the training and the shows. In Longford we had a garage which we turned into a crystal showroom, the dining room downstairs was changed to a healing room, and we had an office upstairs. It was a nice functional house to work from in a quiet, peaceful area situated on the outskirts of the town.

Two stories stick in my mind from that period. One morning I woke up in a state of elation. I had never experienced this feeling before in my life. I was on a tremendous high. The next moment, I received a phone call from a paramedic telling me that my beautiful brother, Marcus, had just passed away. After I recovered from this bolt out of the blue, I realised that the elation I felt was his message to me that his pain was now over. In spite of this, I was devastated and heartbroken. Yet another brother to die in his mid-forties.

After the deaths of my two other brothers, Joey and Johnny, Marcus had hit the bottle, until eventually his whole life revolved around drink. This incredibly talented young man, a wonderful musician, and a gifted singer – he was a trained tenor – had left us. He and I had played together as kids, fought each other, schemed together, and had danced together. He was the one I forced to stay awake at night when I was a child and fearful of spirits. Gone. Just like that.

The funeral was delayed because some members of the family were on holidays abroad, and we had to wait on their return. As it happened, I had a show in Limerick that Sunday and I did think of cancelling it. But what else would I have been doing? So I went along with Pam to the show. I sold the crystals, and Pam attended to the aura camera. As synchronicity would have it, the first person to the stall that morning was a young woman. The first words out of her mouth were: 'I don't know what to do. I've just lost my brother.'

At that moment my need didn't matter, but to be honest I could have done without that happening just right then.

During his drinking phase, Marcus was sometimes very low in spirits. On one of these days, he asked me to play 'The Last Rose of Summer' on the tin whistle at his funeral, whenever that might be. There is a lot of sadness in the song.

> ''Tis the last rose of summer
> Left blooming alone;
> All her lovely companions
> Are faded and gone;
> No flower of her kindred
> No rosebud is nigh
> To reflect back her blushes
> To give sigh for sigh.'

I play by ear, and the lyrics always run through my mind as I play the melody. The first two lines on the next verse, 'I'll not leave thee, thou lone one! To pine on the stem' almost broke my heart when I tried to play the tune leading up to the funeral. Those words brought me such pain and loneliness and I could not hold back the tears.

I will never forget how tough it was to play that tune on the day of the funeral. The church in Dalkey is old and quaint, with an organ upstairs. That was where we went to play music and sing during the Mass. By this stage I'd figured out that if I tried to play the tune on my own I would not be able to. Then I remembered: when Pam and I did healings we said a prayer beforehand that calls in God and the angels for help and protection. So before I played the song, I did that. As it happened, at the very moment I was to start playing, one of Marcus' old teachers fainted in the church, which resulted in a delay of the ceremony for a few minutes. This meant I had to stand there and wait longer than expected. But when I finally played the tune I was able to get through it perfectly. I was so relieved.

At his burial my intention was to play the tune 'The Minstrel Boy'. The lyrics start with, 'The minstrel boy to the war has gone, in the ranks of death you will find him.' However, this time I had forgotten to say the prayer for protection, and as I thought of the words while starting to play I found myself weeping. At that moment the sense of loss became a reality too hard to carry and I couldn't continue playing.

For a while afterwards I was angry and upset about his passing. I found it really hard to let him go. Then, about a week after his month's mind (a requiem Mass that is celebrated about a month after a person's death in memory of the deceased), I felt the same elation as I experienced on the day of his death. I knew it was Marcus trying to make me understand it was time to say goodbye and let him go, and to try to live on. So I sat down and said my own special prayers that help spirits find peace, and let my lovely brother go Home. I know I will carry that pain for life, but what alleviates it are the cherished memories I will always have of the happy times we had together.

Soon after that Pam and I did a show in Killarney. I noticed a woman looking at me as I worked with the crystals. She came over, said she liked me and handed me a light green crystal which looked like polished quartz. As she asked me if I knew what it was, I felt the crystal's energy race through my body.

I said I wasn't sure, but it looked a bit like peridot. When she told me it was prehnite, I was really surprised. I had a piece of prehnite that had travelled with me from the first time we bought crystals as part of the stock, but its finish was more like chalky selenite than quartz. But I knew as soon as I felt her crystal I had to work with it. It became obvious that this lady worked with crystals. I held up my own piece of prehnite to compare it energetically with hers, and accidentally dropped my crystal on the ground, where it broke into three pieces. It rattled the hell out of me when I picked it back up, because its energy went right through my body and I felt the same sensation I'd got when the lady handed me her prehnite. After letting me hold her crystal for a few more moments she took it back and left. I never saw her ever again.

I put my prehnite in my pocket and, over the next week and a half, held the fragmented crystal as often as I could in my receiving hand, my left hand. Every time I did I could feel the energy of the crystal traverse my body, until it highlighted painful emotions I was carrying. This manifested as a physical pain in my spleen. This demonstrates the power of crystals and how well they work. The pain grew in intensity until I knew I had to do something about it. I asked Pam to fix me and got up on the plinth in absolute agony. But after the healing I actually felt worse.

Pam said she could not get rid of my pain, but felt I'd know the cause of it over the next two or three days. She was right. I went to my nephew's 21st birthday party that weekend and my sister-in-law asked me if I was sure I should be doing this spiritual work, as it often kept me away from home and this upset my mum and the rest of my family a lot. I calmly answered, 'Absolutely. I am in the right place doing the right thing. It is what I was created to do.' The pain disappeared immediately. This proved God works in mysterious ways, and you always need to listen and be present to Him. In those moments I took back my power. I didn't let the judgements or views of others control me like I used to do in the past, and this was a very valuable learning.

In reviewing our time in Longford, I was very focused on one-to-one work with many clients as well as doing workshops and the shows. Pam had shown tremendous commitment to the twin flames, and I know in her mind she felt I was dragging my heels regarding moving to Longford. So often I felt I had let her down. However, we met some fantastic people at that time. They included two lads who helped us move all the healing centre materials and Pam' belongings to Longford, several women who greatly supported us, and of course the clients. But it wasn't long before things were to change again.

As we go through life we often experience real trauma, but like the phoenix and with the help of Spirit we rise up and fly again. The synchronicity of meeting that crystal healer in Killarney that day and the release of the pain at the 21st was part of my learning and was created by divine will. I had no hand, act or part in creating it. All I had to do was be present and trust in the guidance of Spirit.

CHAPTER 13

Further West

When we could, Pam and I used to take some time out and enjoy sacred space on Achill. As we walked the beach on Keel one day I said, 'It is very hard to hold the energy of the twin flames in Longford. Maybe if we could find a space here, we could bring the centre home to where our spiritual journey started.' I was talking about some time in the future, but once again it would not be long before divine providence took a hand in moving us on quicker than I had expected.

Perhaps it was divine prompting, or an eventual recognition of Pam's desperate unhappiness in Longford, or maybe it was also an understanding of the negative impact that Pam's longing for her soul home was having on our spiritual connection. No one should live their life in unhappiness and Pam being separated from Achill was like her oxygen had been taken away. To be honest, I knew she only lived in Greystones, Blackrock and Longford because she trusted the Boss to guide her, and she always did what He told her.

While Pam had a longing to be back on Achill, I still didn't feel ready to leave my home in Dublin and join her despite all the signs urging me to do so. My resistance had not yet been fully broken.

I was, even now, fearful about the future and reluctant to trust that my plan and God's plan were the same. The fear felt like I was being asked to jump out of a plane without a parachute and being told God would catch me. Pam would say, 'God's teaching you to trust Him, Gerry. When you do, God will give us what we need.' This felt almost like a reminder that my lack of trust was holding us back and preventing the inevitable success that God wanted to give us. Pam wanted an ascetic lifestyle, but I felt I was not cut out for that. Pam wanted stillness, and I was the storm.

If Pam really wanted to do something, it would get done incredibly quickly. I shouldn't have been surprised when, within two weeks, she had found a place on Achill. God, the angels and Pam working together – what a powerful combination. The house that Pam found was designed and built by an architect who was very empathic with nature. The shape of the house reminded me of the pyramids of Giza and had definite echoes of my Egyptian past life. It didn't take me long to realise the connection was no mistake. Within a short space of time we were packing our bags and moving the healing centre to Achill. Pam was going back to her soul home.

As with Longford, Pam thought I was going to live in the centre with her, but that thought was short-lived. My hope was that Pam would be happy back in Achill, and she definitely was – and I would be able to live in Dublin and continue to protect Jean and the children. I was still trying to do the balancing act that would see me holding my family together while working in Achill when I could. I sort of didn't get, 'Thy will, not my will, be done.'

It was a real tug of war between God and me. I was like the Jews of old, who fought God to get what they wanted. God likes a good fight. Remember your man, Jacob, who wrestled with the angel all night? He would not let the angel go until he gave him something. Ha ha, he got renamed Israel. Incredible. The gift of my journey with all its pain and struggle was to learn how to let go of the past and trust people again. After a difficult childhood and many difficult events as a young adult, I had lost faith and belief in people and myself. When I awakened, to quote Vicky Wall, 'I began to see the rainbow through my tears.'

Once again, our friends put their backs into helping us move; there was no delay. One day we were in Longford, and the next day in Achill. Pam did not hang around. Work started on making this centre a place for people to come to and touch stillness and peace. We also continued to bring the aura imaging camera to angel shops and both the crystals and camera to holistic shows around the country. A newsletter promoting our workshops and courses on Achill was produced and distributed far and wide. To make all these changes we applied to the bank for a loan. The bank looked over our accounts and, seeing we had not missed payments on previous loans, gave approval straight away. As it happened, this was the time that money was being given out by banks like confetti. Those were the days!

It was the journeys by car that were the greatest drain on

our resources. Now Pam and I had to drive two hours further than before to do any work that involved travelling off the island. Added to that, petrol prices were on the rise, which didn't help. We were going to have to work extra hard just to survive. By now we were used to the pressure and had made progress, so anything was possible.

Pam hoped that as the centre became better known, people would come to us, vastly reducing the need to work away in different venues across the country. I hoped for this too, but didn't believe in this as much as Pam did. It is true to say that we did have some people arrive at our doors in strange ways, people who were guided to us. For me it was time for God to honour the phrase, 'Build it and they will come.'

I brought up the suggestion again of creating an outreach programme with healing clinics around the country. I felt this could lead to a stronger client base, but Pam was still not in favour of it.

When we left for Longford we still had to travel to Dublin to continue client sessions, so we rented a small room in Loughlinstown. Unfortunately that venue didn't prove successful. Then for a while we worked from a room in a house in Cabinteely owned by friends of ours, and eventually we settled in a room in the Stillorgan Park Hotel, now the Talbot Hotel Stillorgan. It was there we stayed and worked with many people down the years. I still work there myself today. Eventually Pam would stop coming to Dublin to work with clients, but for now she continued coming to Stillorgan with me.

The house in Achill had just enough room to accommodate the needs of the centre. The house was open plan and was split by a wall into two clearly defined areas. We set up a little shop in the conservatory, and the kitchen/living room area provided a space for us to hold various trainings. We also had a beautiful healing room at the end of a long hall. There was also an outhouse, half of which was made available to us for our printing equipment and for storing and preparing the crystals for the shows.

On the day we moved the centre to Achill, I had the feeling that at some time in the future I would live there. I stood in the tower part of the building and looked around. A cold shiver ran up and down my spine, anticipation of what was to come. The fact that we were now based here on the island went against all business practicality of 'location location location', but spiritually this place felt like a piece of heaven. I tried to hold onto the hope that people would come to the island for retreats and workshops.

Suddenly I became distracted by something outside. I saw a man trying to push back a growth of weeds and rough grass edging a driveway that was made from a lot of gravel loosely spread over the soil. It was pretty much a hapless effort on his part. This really was a place where nature was in charge. Mother nature was our gardener with the wild beauty of the natural world all around.

We knew the Internet would be a great help in promoting the centre. This proved a little more difficult than first anticipated. The area we worked from now was remote, and about three people shared one phone line. Also, the Internet on Achill wasn't broadband by any stretch of the imagination. For example, sometimes we would need information from the US about our aura camera, so Pam would crank up the old computer and leave it on overnight in the hope that it would be finished sending our email message when we woke up in the morning. Fast mail, how are ye! After a bit of research and advice we got a dongle. We asked a computer technician who was used to the communication problems on Achill how well it would work. He said, 'As long as you're facing the mast you should be OK.' And that's how we did it, and it did help. It didn't resolve the problem but it was better than nothing.

One evening, shortly after moving the centre to Achill, I thought it might be nice to get a takeaway. When I asked Pam where the nearest fish and chip shop was she looked at me, amused. 'They are closed for the winter,' she said. 'They only open in the summer for the tourist season. McDonald's is about an hour away in Castlebar, if you want drive that far.'

I was crestfallen. Of course I couldn't expect things to be as available here as they were in Dublin. This jackeen had a lot to learn about rural life. But I couldn't say a bad word about the place. The island was absolutely stunning. Pam and I had a favourite beach, Keem beach. The sea had moments of peaceful splendour when the sun glistened on turquoise waters, and at other times it was full of white horses and amazingly powerful waves. Life is at a more measured pace there, and Pam was at home in this bucolic setting. You'd often see her drinking in her Achill like it was nectar of the gods.

The people there are special, different. Even though there is a bridge connecting Achill to the mainland, they are still very much an island people. Rumour has it that if they don't like you they'd put you on the far shore and swing the bridge, blocking your return. (The Michael Davitt Bridge on Achill was constructed so that it could be swung to open the waterway whenever needed.) You could mostly get what you needed in the Sound, a village on the east coast of Achill island, and the settlement closest to the mainland. The nearest large town on the mainland is Castlebar, which is the gateway to the rest of the country and about an hour away. Westport, slightly smaller in size, is a thriving picturesque town with a beautiful energy and is just a little closer to Achill than Castlebar.

The landscape there changes with the seasons and Achill could put a new face on for each time of the day. Sometimes the mist hangs over Sliabh Mór, one of Achill's mountains. During those times you could see her majesty lift her head to the clouds. I learned that long ago in Achill there was a bustling village situated at the foot of Sliabh Mór. Its population was devastated by the Great Famine, and all that's left now are ruins. It is known as the deserted village, and is a constant reminder of those who passed and emigrated, a sad requiem to the island's past.

The roads are made for a more leisurely pace of life, and the only traffic jams to be seen were when sheep decided to sit in the centre of the road. This was a frequent occurrence, and it was funny to see the animals eyeballing the cars as if they were the masters of the road and the humans' metal machines were just a nuisance. As we settled in we found a lovely B&B to look after our guests and clients, and the owner of the house typified the hospitality of the island's inhabitants.

∾

Pam had always wanted a labyrinth, and now she had an opportunity to create one. You could not have picked a more beautiful vista; it was as if God made it specially for us. Part of the land outside our house led to the sea and there the water twisted and turned, ebbed and flowed serpent-like around numerous little banks and islets. In the distance you could see the mountains, and we felt this would be an ideal backdrop to the proposed installation.

We acquired four strong stones about three feet high, and they were placed like sentinels at the edges of a square piece of land we dedicated to the labyrinth. The stones all had a shape uncannily close to the outline of the Madonna. Within the square we placed five pathways created by smaller stones on loose gravel. These pathways in this beautiful setting would be ideal for meditation, prayer and quiet reflection. We were very pleased with the final result. We agreed it was an amazing construction, and you could really feel and breathe in the stillness when you were within it. It was certainly a winner when we held workshops. We noticed that whenever a person passed through the labyrinth, its energy increased. We even had quite a few visits from a number of local people who liked to walk the labyrinth, carrying their thoughts and feelings as they strolled the pathways of pilgrimage.

The centre had a life of its own. One day I asked Pam if there was any link between Giza in Egypt and the house. She said she didn't know. Then about six weeks later we were given the gift of a book called *The Sacred Whore*. It talked about sacred places in Ireland and claimed that a ley line from Giza came out at Croagh Patrick, a well-known mountain and pilgrimage site in Mayo, and quite close to Achill. I have to admit I never really had to wait too long for answers to come to my spiritual questions.

We rarely worked less than sixty hours a week and sometimes

more. Apart from attending clinics and travelling to shows, at the centre we held workshops, prepared crystals for the shows, wrote up booklets, promotional leaflets and were always printing and updating information. There were days we could start at five o'clock in the morning and not go to bed until two the following morning.

However, there was always some time to appreciate the beauty of nature all around. As a kid I had loved trees and plants and the sea, and used to write a lot of nature poems. Over the years, though, through work and other commitments I had lost touch with that part of me. But now, being on Achill, my love of nature was reawakened, and I will forever be grateful for that.

Here are a few experiences I had from my observations of animals on Achill. It was here I learned greater empathy for God's creatures and a better understanding of their intelligence. One day two cows and two calves were in a field chewing the cud. From the window I noticed that one calf was bullying the other one. The mother went up and clattered her errant child with her head as much as to say, 'Leave her alone.' I thought of our own mothers, and how they would do the same. It all looked so relatable.

Another day I noticed two sheep standing still, near the house. Their heads were cocked to one side, and it was only when the shepherd arrived a little while later to round them up did I realise they had been listening out and waiting for him. When the man came up to them, they legged it and led him a merry dance around the house. Eventually they won and the shepherd had to leave them be until another day. It taught me that animals know a lot more than we think they know.

We had a cattle grid at the front gate and one day we saw a sheep roll over the grid, like a marine in training, to get in to graze at the grass in our garden. Who said sheep aren't clever? Another nugget of information I gleaned on Achill was that a ewe bleats a lot when her little lamb is taken away from her by a human. But if a fox gets the lamb, there is a lot less bleating. She seems to understand that 'it is what it is', that it is nature taking its course.

We were also visited by goats, who preferred to look at us side on instead of straight in the eye. They were curious animals, and often stood on our low windowsills and peeped in the windows at us. We used to wonder what they were thinking! Among their group was a beautiful chocolate brown baby goat, who couldn't get enough of standing on the sill and watching us as we went about our daily business.

Bird lovers would have been in their element in Achill. We had lots of bird feeders outside the house and we watched birds of all kinds feeding and flying around. The island was alive with life and beauty was everywhere.

∽

By December 2008 I still had not moved onto Achill. I was just about holding the family together, although this was not going to last much longer. The twin flames were going to live together in this lifetime and even though I didn't know it yet, the battle was almost lost.

CHAPTER 14

The Last Straw

My relationship was now severely in decline with Jean. I was not home often enough and the work I was doing was suffocating our connection. We still loved each other but relationships need to be worked on and no matter how hard I tried, I am sure the lost time felt like abandonment to her. When I spent what time I could back in the family home, they all talked to me about what was going on, but no one seemed to see things from my perspective, or how hard I was fighting to survive. Pressure was coming from all sides. How could they understand? This was a horrible price I was paying for the path I had to walk.

If anything went wrong, and it frequently did, both Pam and my family would be left struggling, sometimes very badly. Travelling back and forth from Achill was one of the main problems as it kept costs very high, but Pam didn't see it that way. She saw my refusal to move to Achill as the principal reason as to why things were so tough for us, and insisted that abundance would come when I surrendered.

Synchronistic events were to be played out coming up to the end of 2008 which changed everything. The crystals had brought us by now essential cash flow and with the aura camera we had a fairly regular income. When you added that to the client work and workshops, we were just about holding our own.

We managed the crystals really well in terms of purchases, and had trade customers who would buy nearly enough of what we brought back from the UK to cover the costs of our trips there. This had worked well up to around August 2008. One of our best customers, a couple who ran a holistic shop in Dublin, bought around €400 worth of crystals from us on a regular basis. It was an order we greatly valued. But this time they couldn't because their backer was pulling out and they were about to close their shop. For us, the loss of this order, along with raising nearly €2,000 for a particular show which turned out to be a disaster, brought a whole new meaning to being tight. Trust again, trust some more. But what more could I do? Hadn't I shown enough trust? I was worried and looked for a solution. I heard fortune favours the brave, and I was about to be either very brave or very foolish, depending on perspective.

The couple who ran the shop came to us with an offer. They asked us if we would be interested in taking over their previous backer's role. According to the couple the shop was just about covering itself. We considered and discussed their offer. The shop was in a good area, with a healing and training room upstairs. If we took it on we could expand the crystal range in the shop, do more training and workshops upstairs and bring along the aura camera as well. We would have a base again in Dublin, and not need to work in the hotel. Another advantage was that we would have far easier access to the biggest population centre in Ireland. But on a personal level the biggest plus was that I could spend more time at home. God had provided me with a way to save my marriage, or so I thought. All in all, the plan seemed ideal and it looked like we could all benefit from working together.

I agonised over the decision for a couple of weeks, but time was of the essence. I sat in the little chapel in Cornelscourt praying and seeking answers. The answer I got was that the Dublin shop could hold an important light where it was. I took that to be a yes. Maybe I wanted a yes, maybe I needed a yes. But first I had to make sure that Pam was in favour of this venture. She agreed and so we told the couple we were happy to invest in the shop.

In taking that approach, I trusted the opportunity without doing due diligence. Looking at the books and going through the shop's accounts would have been prudent and businesslike, but by now I was desperate to prove I could be spiritual and trust in divine providence. I was happy to take the risk because I thought that God and I had the same plan and that a positive outcome would be assured. I didn't realise that this would be the final break in my resistance to moving from Dublin, revealing a different divine plan than I had in my head.

To raise the money to secure the shop I decided to borrow from my credit union close on €20,000 which would be necessary to take the shop over and stock it better. Of course my challenge as ever was trust, so I was determined this time to change my ways and believe in people.

We brought in more stock and refurbished the place, but there was trouble in the camp from the start. The price quoted for the rent was €300 less than the actual rent, which was €1,300 per month. The turnover had also been overstated. Then there was a clash of ethos with Pam, as she refused to sell any Indian or shamanic memorabilia, even though the shop had a clientele who loved these products. I suppose my business head was open to allowing the shop to continue the way it had in the past with the previous owners. I thought it should be inclusive, not exclusive. But from where Pam was coming from, spiritually there was no option as she would have found it impossible to support a venture that wasn't Christ-centred. The name of the shop had to be changed, and there was discord over that as well. With each of these changes came a level of bitterness and resentment from the two people we had trusted. They felt we had gazumped their business, but they needed the money and felt pressure to comply. They became very unwilling partners.

Ireland was heading into a deep recession and at one stage during this time the euro and sterling almost reached parity. People started to go up north for their Christmas shopping in droves. This strangled the retail trade nationwide, which included our little shop.

We introduced a cash register and some basic professional stock control and management, which was resisted by the other couple. I was good with stock and it became obvious that the level of goods leaving the premises did not match the purported income, and profit margins were non-existent. Even though we followed business protocol to track stock loss, we never found out where the missing stock went. The realisation began to dawn that a venture I thought would be a great help to us was becoming a terrible burden, and Pam and I became more and more stressed with the issues related to both the shop and the partners.

Around that time Pam had to go into hospital for tests. The guys Upstairs probably knew she needed rest. But the Mind Body Spirit show in the RDS was coming up and it was essential that Pam was there to operate the camera. She was allowed out of the hospital on her absolute promise that she would return nightly at a set time. This shows the full level of madness that existed then. Imagine taking a woman out of her sick bed and making her work. Pam had decided on this herself, but I don't think it made me popular with her friends. In their eyes – with the limited knowledge they had – I was being cruel, and that was not the case.

Eventually we had to call a halt to the mess surrounding the shop, and we suggested taking over running the retail part on our own. This meant the couple would not be involved in the day-to-day running of the shop at all, and would just do their healing work upstairs. On the day of that discussion they agreed, but a day later they told us we were robbing them of their shop and being nasty to them. In situations like this it is the truth that is often the victim.

I didn't have time for a nervous breakdown. We were fast approaching the Christmas period and hoped the turnover during this time would help to improve things and ease the pressure. Pam and I were continuing to work with the camera and were also doing some training. In early December we opened a stall in Blackrock market, a long-running market carrying a broad range of goods, and stocked it by splitting the stock in the shop and staffing the market stall with unpaid volunteers. Friends and family stepped in and worked for nothing to keep it going. I will always be grateful for the help they gave us then, as this really was a desperate time.

A couple of weeks before Christmas we parked the black goddess outside the shop while we did a full day of aura camera photos upstairs. As we had a crystal training class scheduled in the shop later that evening, we loaded the car up with the camera equipment at six o'clock so we could leave promptly after the crystal training was over. Just as the class started, we heard banging on the bins outside the shop. We didn't realise the noise of the bins was actually to cloak the damage that was being done to our car as a group of young lads tried to rob it. So when I looked out the window and saw to my horror that the car was being attacked, I rushed downstairs and outside only to see the lads running from the car with their arms full of our equipment.

God knows how much we lost that day, but because I remembered a robbery that happened to a family member, we actually ended up having a small bit of luck. My brother's house had been broken into on a few occasions. On one of those times we decided to search the grounds around where he lived and in doing so, found his television. The robbers had left the telly hidden in the undergrowth to come back for later. Remembering this, I searched the waste ground behind the car park with another course participant. To our relief, we found a lot of the bits needed for the operation of the aura system, but the computer was gone. At least we still had the discs and the bio sensor, and just enough of the essential aura equipment required for us to be able to operate the system. We had to replace the camera and computer, buy a new printer, reload the system and in time we were up and running again – if you could call it that.

The shop lost us €30,000 in approximately three months. It was a nightmare. You could not script what was happening. Pam would always ask me to look at the positives, but in those moments I could not see one. Both of us were heavily in debt and under severe pressure. Something had to give. We had no choice but to close the shop and remove all our stock from it as Christmas trading came to an end.

One night just before Christmas, as I lay beside my lovely wife, I felt a coldness and distance between us that I'd never felt before. Sadly, I knew then that I had finally lost her. Despite all my efforts, I had failed to hold us together, and I knew it wasn't right to keep her in pain over this whole situation any more. I cried myself silently to sleep, realising that God had won and I had to move to Achill.

It so happened that I had some work to do at the healing centre in Achill, so I drove there in the black car. I then needed to drive the estate to Dublin to gather up our goods from the stall in the Blackrock market and the shop in Dublin. On arrival in Dublin I loaded the car with all the stock from the shop so I could hand back the keys and leave that place for good. Then I went to the Blackrock market and emptied out the stall. The short-lived adventure with retail was over, and so was my resistance.

After that I headed down to Cork. Some time before, Jean

and I planned to spend Christmas with Jean's mother in Cork, but with all the changed plans Jean and I got diverted to stay with my daughter Emma and my son-in-law Joe just outside Cork city, about twenty minutes from my mother-in-law's place. Jean travelled on her own by bus to her mother's house and then Emma collected her from there and brought her to her own house. When I arrived at Emma's house I was met by Joe. I remember it was a cold Christmas that year in more ways than one. Joe showed me into a guest room, and I realised it was the first time since I got married that I was to sleep at night without my wife by my side when we were in the same location. Still, we did all meet up for breakfast the next day and Christmas came and went peacefully enough.

Pam and I had two Reiki trainings booked on Achill for January. It was really great to be able to do the work and feel you were making a real contribution to people's lives, but it was also a blessing we had the bookings because without them we wouldn't have survived.

But before I left Cork for Achill I knew I had to speak to Jean. Telling her I had to leave her was one of the hardest things I ever had to do. I was so disconnected from myself that I'd forgotten it was her dad's anniversary that day. Jean said we'd talk about it when we were both back in Dublin – me from Achill and Jean from Cork.

After the Reiki trainings in Achill, I came back to Dublin to collect my things, and to confirm to Jean that I was not coming back. I could not fix this and anything I had tried only made matters worse. I was so focused on making my words as clear and definite as I could so my precious Jean could now move on in life but again, I wasn't thinking straight. It happened to be Valentine's Day, of all days, when I told her. Things couldn't have got any worse. I really had done enough damage. She came over, sat beside me and held my hand. My heart was breaking. She did not deserve this. We were meant to be together for life, Gerry and Jean. In that moment I fell apart inside as I remembered a lifetime of love and support. I was aware she'd never really know how hard I fought for her, but it didn't matter now. I had still failed.

It wasn't long before the news spread among the family. I knew my mum was devastated that I had separated from Jean, and I had nothing to say to her when she tried in vain to order her errant son back home. She never forgave me, and I heard her anger, hurt and sadness in every word she spoke to me from then on. She never knew how much I grieved over the whole situation.

When I finally moved to Achill, it was not with a sense of awe and wonder, but rather with resignation. I could not have taken any more. I was sick in my heart and in my stomach, and part of me didn't want to live. As things were right then, I couldn't support my wife and children because I had no money left. I had spent six years fighting to hold it together. Six years of stress, loss and poverty. Six years of trusting that God would look after me and my family. I dearly hoped that God was going to deliver now, and I would be able to support my family from afar. I had nothing left to lose.

There was a strange sense of relief that the war was over. God had prepared the way for me and my resistance was gone. We had a good house on Achill and now it was time for clients to come. I never thought that things would be simple, but now I really needed a break. I had gone through my own personal tsunami, and had taken all the losses I could.

It was all divine timing. I was finally going to live and work with my twin flame on Achill. A new life was about to begin.

∾

It wasn't long before the couple in Dublin who had betrayed us had drawn another two people into working with them at their shop, and that ended up in much the same mess.

But something good came out of that debacle. All of a sudden, instead of blaming everyone else for my misfortune and believing that people couldn't be trusted, I became aware that the journey up to date had strengthened me, and I put the blame where it needed to be, on myself. I accepted responsibility for it and moved on. I had developed a greater clarity and realised that although I had trusted and been let down, I would be able to trust again, and would also be able to have more belief and hope in people in the future too.

CHAPTER 15

Surrender

My life was in God's hands now but I didn't know if I really was in calmer waters or just in the eye of the storm. By this stage we had created good groundwork for the healing centre. Along with always watching our pennies Pam and I did our best to work together as harmoniously as we could. I had also undergone a high degree of spiritual surrender. However, the wars we had been through had taken some of the shine off the twin flames. Pam had a few more health challenges at this time, and possibly her stoicism and my focus on survival meant I sometimes didn't see the extent of struggle and pain she endured. To this day she is a real fighter and one could only be proud of her determination and strength. By and large we took the knocks together and stood by each other, but by the start of 2009 we were both a bit weary.

Trouble was never far away and in January of that year the banks decided to withdraw our overdraft facility and turned it into a term loan. We had not done anything wrong; it was just about the banks redirecting credit during a time of nationwide economic collapse. This added another amount to our payments every month and starved us of our flexibility.

We also had to deal with the wear and tear on the cars which had been a constant nightmare. When we moved to Achill Pam had the black goddess and I had the trusty Ford Focus. I know now that they should have been serviced more regularly, which could have prevented some of the serious mechanical problems that occurred. Nonetheless, several of our cars had been problematic from the start.

The black estate car continued to give us grief. So when we were going to the shops one day and the engine warning light flashed up on the dashboard again and stayed flashing this time, I took the car straight away to Pam's friendly mechanic.

'Oh, it's that computer glitch again,' he said. 'You'll be fine.'

I kept on driving, and it wasn't long before it all went horribly wrong. The car's turbo blew. The warning had not been a computer glitch, and the car should have been checked out and fixed. The damage done was going to take a lot of money we didn't have to fix it, so that meant coming up with a plan. We arranged to trade in my Ford Focus with the mechanic. This way we were able to pay for a new turbo for the black car and I bought another second-hand car (which was not cheap) from the mechanic. I never saw so many things going wrong in my life at the same time, but I'm sure that God had His reasons.

Our repayments went up and this put extra strain on both of us. By now petrol and diesel prices were going through the roof. Ireland's economy was in free fall, and Achill seemed even further away from the people we needed to reach. Then out of the blue we were contacted by a supplier we had in the UK with whom we had developed a really good business relationship. He offered us a range of crystal jewellery and told us that we could have it on sale or return. I wasn't sure about this at all. I didn't want any more financial commitments. However, we agreed and got the jewellery in to mix with the crystals. Thankfully the jewellery seemed to shore things up a little. It was harder now than ever to bring people for weekends to Achill, but we soldiered on. I don't know how, but the why was more important. We absolutely believed that God would somehow carry us through.

The island was now my adopted home and I was starting to get used to the way of life there. I do think Pam got the odd giggle as she introduced her Achill to this Dub. No matter what anyone says, it definitely was an adventure and a place where I learned to appreciate the beauty of nature. Even though my own soul home is Dublin, I also have a deep affection for Achill and the people of the island. What follows are just some of the mixed bag of experiences I had on Achill around this time.

You could see the stars in Achill in a way you rarely see them in Dublin. They were so beautiful and bright. Because I was so familiar with the presence of streetlights in Dublin, it took a while to get used to the darkness in Achill at night-time. The first night I spent there it was so dark I thought there was a power cut! And if we were ever returning by car to our house late in the evening, we had to let the headlights shine on the door so we could see where the keyhole was.

I remember driving home one night among the star-studded skies whilst listening to a local radio programme. The person being interviewed was talking about hosting a stargazing festival in the area, and there was no denying Achill would be an ideal place, as there was little or no light pollution on the island.

I knew there were plenty of nature spirits around in this beautiful, pure and rural corner of Ireland, and I was careful to respect their wild places. I had not actually met any, but due to my evolving awareness I could sense when they were around. One time I came out of the house and looked at our wild garden. I had recently heard local people talk about the murder of the hedgerows with bushwhacker machines, and how some sensitive people could hear screams of pain from the bushes. I said to the fairies in the garden: 'It's all right, lads. You can let the weeds grow as much as you want. I doubt I'll be creating a manicured garden with pruned bushes anytime soon.' They seemed to take me at my word. I've never seen nettles grow so tall. Be careful what you wish for! You might just receive more than you expect.

It was funny, when I moved into that house first I swore I would never sleep there alone. I was not used to quiet spaces and you could not have got quieter than that place. It sounds like I was being a big girl's blouse, but the place was remote and hey, I'm a Dub. On a weekend when Pam was away teaching a workshop, I remembered the big teddy bear she used regularly on inner child courses. So me and the teddy bear went to bed together, and I slept the night through. I actually learned a lot from that experience. I discovered that I should be kinder to myself and not be afraid to go and get what my body and soul needed whenever necessary. I also knew from then on I could survive being in the house on my own, and my fear about that lessened greatly over time.

There is a great community spirit amongst the people of Achill and down the years we made some lovely friends. Now and again, at events in the local hall, we got a chance to exhibit the work we did at the centre, which included crystal healing, colour therapy and healing sessions. We would also have a wide variety of crystals on display. It wasn't just adults who attended – many young people came along as well. The children were especially drawn to our crystals, and were delighted to be introduced to the wonders and magic of the crystal energy.

We were always trying to promote the centre and so we created a sign with a photograph of the house and details about it on a large corrugated board, and took the sign with us to shows and fairs around the country. The picture showed the house nestled in the wild and natural environment of Achill. We had a relatively open tenancy and as the house was doing what it was built for and we were friends with the owner, we knew we could trust her and our residency.

After displaying the sign many times, one day in the South Court Hotel show in Limerick a psychic reader looked at the sign and pointed out that he could see the head of a nature spirit in the garden. We examined the photo, and sure enough, within a collage of twigs, flowers and leaves we saw the unmistakable head of the Green Man himself laughing gaily. Spanning back thousands of years, the Green Man is believed to be a spirit of nature personified as a man. As more people noticed the face, the picture started to change. The plants gained a visible aura, and you could see energy lifting off them and off the roof of the house as well. At one stage there was a discernible human head visible just over the house. We even had visitors from Egypt in the photo, which included a big black dog which looked very much like the Egyptian god Anubis. Strange times indeed.

One day, Pam and I were scheduled to do a healing in the house. At that same time, two friends from Dublin came to visit and we discussed the possibility of us all working together and developing a community for healers and therapists in the centre. I was feeling quite sorry for myself at that time, not wanting to be there at all, and when Pam and I went down to the client to do the healing, the visitors talked amongst themselves in the kitchen-cum-living room. They had noticed my irritation with everything and questioned the validity of the twin flames. All of a sudden the flame of the candle on the table repeated the same amazing thing that happened some time before – it split in two and came back to one, and then repeated this again and again. One of our friends was quick enough to record the phenomenon on his phone, and later forwarded the video to me. I have it on my phone to this day.

It was later on the same day that I looked outside and saw an angel hovering on the far side of the window. It was not big, but you could clearly see the wings and the light body. Most people would go, 'Wow!' I said, 'Please don't come in. I promise I'll be good, I promise I'll do what you've asked.' With that, the whole sky filled with these beings of light, and I felt suitably admonished, like I knew I had been a bold little boy. I got the message, which was: 'Grow up and do the work you were created to do.' Even though they were aware I was unhappy about a lot of things, they were letting me know it was time for me to give up moaning.

One part of my journey that made me smile every now and then was the idea of being an elemental, a leprechaun to be precise. I'd met people doing healing work who were convinced I was one, and gradually the idea that I had a past life as a leprechaun gained traction. The more I let go of my rational world the more I moved into a broader consciousness where life is different and we are more than we can ever imagine. At training and in the clinics I had been absolutely privileged to meet a number of people who told me they had been elves in a past life. They were happy with their elf-like features and sense of humour and fun. I also met a lot of gentle little souls who saw themselves as fairies, and a number of ladies and gents that had a shape and stature similar to mine, who claimed to be leprechauns.

On the first trip that took me to Achill, as we were driving along Pam pointed out the cottage where Tanis Helliwell, author of *Summer with the Leprechauns*, met a leprechaun. Pam had given me the book to read some time back and I had found it a little unusual and funny. But who was I to say that what the woman experienced was not real? The story had really valuable teachings about humans' interactions with the natural world, and attempts of the elementals to learn about humans and teach them about the elemental kingdom.

So even though I did not dismiss the possibility of being an elemental, it was to be some time before I really accepted it.

On one occasion I was asked by Spirit to bring the special holy waters of the triple goddess Maid, Mother and Crone together. We already had a good supply from a holy well that was connected to Pam. This well represented the Mother. I asked my son if he would accompany me to collect the waters from the other two wells, and he said he'd be happy do so. Our first stop was Bridget's well, which represented the Maid, in County Kildare. As it happened, that day the only money I had was a €50 note which I planned to spend on fuel for the car. We arrived at the well and I bent down and scooped up the water in a jar. In hindsight I admit I wasn't mindful or reverent enough whilst doing this sacred task. Soon after, we drove to the garage to put diesel in the car but when I put my hand in my pocket to take out the €50, it was gone. To say I was a bit distressed was an understatement. But something told me to return to the well and give thanks and show respect. I went back and there was the €50 on the ground beside the well. I knew in my heart I had been told to behave.

The next stop was the Hill of Tara. There we would look for Maebh's well, containing the water of the Crone. Some of these wells are really hard to find, and Maebh's well seemed to be one of these. However, we did come across St Patrick's well, where serendipity was to play a part. I remembered information in the book that had been given to Pam that claimed a ley line came all the way from Giza to Croagh Patrick. This book also told the story of the Hag's (also known as the Crone's) well, whose name was Maebh.

When my son and I read the Meath County Council sign in front of St Patrick's well it said this particular well had many names down the centuries. Legend said that Conchobar mac Nessa drank from the well after sleeping with the Hag there, after which he became King of all Ireland. So this meant we were actually at the right place; in finding the Hag's name associated with this well, we knew it had to be Maebh's well.

So with all the waters collected, we brought Maid Mother and Crone together in equal measure. We were then told to place these holy waters in the centre of our labyrinth for three days around the full moon. This was to energise the water. After a while the water became olive green and in Aura-Soma olive green is about feminine leadership. I thought that was fascinating, as this signified the unification of the triple goddesses.

At a time when the world is moving into honouring the divine feminine, it was interesting that I, a man, was asked to do this task. I really felt this was to do with individuation and the balance of the male and the female within us all. This quest was a journey of trust, and of doing what we were told to do. This special holy water was also used in the centre and given to our friends as well.

∾

On one of my first visits to Achill some years previously, during one of the weekends Pam and I were together, she took me to visit Bartra beach. Just at the water's edge I saw a rock. It looked like it was inscribed with Ogham writing, and I had a sudden intuition about it. I said, 'That rock is from Atlantis.'

Pam said, 'Take it with you.'

It was a decent weight and I wasn't sure if I could carry it to the car. But where there is a will there is a way, and after lugging it for a bit and resting for a bit several times, I eventually got it into the back of the car. We took it back to the house in Achill where it remained for a while and as Pam and I moved the healing centre to different locations over the ensuing years, she took the stone with her. It never seemed to be anything but an ordinary piece of rock until I joined Pam to live in Achill in January 2009.

I put symbols of world religions around the house to show everyone was welcome equally with lots of love and non-judgement. Then we placed the Atlantis rock at the front door. One day, as I came back into the house after getting groceries, I tripped and nearly banged my nose on the stone. Well, that certainly got my attention! That particular weekend we were doing a spiritual workshop, and I noticed that two people didn't seem to be fully engaged and present. I was reminded of the rock, and got the two people to sit beside each other with their feet on it. I wondered if anything would happen, and it certainly did. They were repelled by each other and became emotional as they remembered a trauma from an Atlantean lifetime. Because of this remembrance they were able to resolve their trauma and heal the old wounds they carried. They were then able to reconnect and fully focus on the workshop.

From then on we would often ask people to put their feet on the rock. Sometimes one person would repel another, and other times individuals would be drawn to each other. All this could be clearly seen in their body language. People variously felt cold, nervous, fearful or joyous. It was amazing to see all the different reactions.

Some say that the Minaun cliffs in Achill had at one time been part of Atlantis. Other sources suggest that the original Atlantis was based just off the African continent. During this time I had an opportunity to go to the Azores to dance. When I arrived there I was surprised when I noticed the similarity of flora between Achill and this place way off the coast of Portugal. When I returned home I measured the distance between the west coast of Ireland and Africa, including taking into account land masses, and thought it might indeed be possible that the two locations had been joined together many thousands of years ago. Maybe sometime in the future we will know more, but for now it's just another interesting and intriguing story.

The island has so much to offer as a holiday venue or spiritual retreat, and without doubt is a place where you can find stillness and peace. I feel privileged to have spent part of my life on Achill and am proud to have made friends with so many good people there. I will never forget the way they supported both Pam and myself during our many challenges.

CHAPTER 16

Gateway work

Prior to meeting Pam and embarking on the healing and spiritual journey, God and the angels had started to prepare me for what was going to happen in the future by opening me up to visits from spirits. What my training gave me was a structured approach to doing the work and working with people. It also gave me a deeper understanding of my pain and the pain in others which helped me enormously in understanding the emotional hurts that spirits carried as they made their transition. It became clear that gateway work was a big part of my spiritual responsibility in this lifetime.

The thought of a deceased relative being an earthbound spirit might invoke fear and distress in people. I do not see it in this way. When you go to bed at night and wake up the next morning you don't remember the passage of time when you sleep. If it weren't for dreams and the time on the clock you might find it hard to accept you were asleep for seven or eight hours. Similarly, these spirits are in a safe suspended sleep-like state since passing. They are very secure and safe and just not fully aware. I wonder with some of them if they were really aware on this side. Some of them loved the oul scratcher, if you know what I mean.

Just like the spiritual world has many mysteries, death also has its mystery. With these spirits, it's like they're in a holding space between this world and the next, which by and large is safe and comfortable for them. I've never felt that they are eternally unhappy. I get the sense that most of the time they feel a slight numbness, like they have been given an anaesthetic. Earthbound spirits make a choice to stay around earth for many different reasons. These can include completing unfinished business or caring for a loved one until it becomes clear that it is time to let go.

The prayers that are used to send them onwards involve cutting ties with things of this life that are holding them back. Sometimes they will tell me what these things are, if I ask and listen for the answer. Once these prayers are said I say a final beautiful prayer to God to take them Home. It is important to note that these prayers can be used for all denominations.

Also, we have to understand that time in spirit is different to human time, for instance, two hundred years might feel like no time at all to an earthbound spirit. In summary, they have to complete whatever needs completion and only then do they feel they can go back towards the light, happy and at peace in their own being. Even in this phase they are held by God and the angels, protected, nurtured and loved.

I have learned a lot in doing this work for the last eighteen years and have been blessed with great teachers both on this side and the other side of life. Archangel Michael is one of my teachers and is in charge of my gateway work. Some of the spirits who have come to me in need of healing have helped me to understand that my clients in the physical world could also have challenges in their spirits, as well as in their minds and bodies.

Spirit always tries very hard to get their messages through to me clearly, but it is still easy to misinterpret something and it may take a bit of effort to understand the communication. I have come a long way from when I first believed I was not good enough to be called to do this work to today where I have accepted my role and am happy to be in God's service. Roma Downey, the actress who played an angel in the TV series *Touched by an Angel*, made a lovely statement in an interview on US television when she said, 'God does not always call the qualified, but qualifies those called.'

On one of my trips to Achill, shortly after being brought together with Pam as twin flames, I was asked to pray for the release of 3,000 earthbound spirits from the time of the Famine. But between one thing and another I kept putting this spiritual request on the long finger. Every time I visited Achill I remembered I had this job to do, and then I went and forgot about it until I went back to Achill again.

This went on for about three years. Eventually one day I said to myself, Here goes, they're going Home. But how was I going to do it? I didn't know. Could I do them all together? But if I did that I might miss one, so I decided to pray for them all individually. 3,000 is a lot of spirits. As I was trying to work things out I got a message from the other side that told me there were now 4,500 waiting for me to send Home. Gee, thanks God. 1,500 more! He was really teaching me patience and obedience.-

I made a numbered list for every spirit so I could keep them all accounted for. Then I went to the healing room, lit a candle, said my opening prayer, called in protection and away I went. After each prayer I asked if the spirit had gone Home and doused with the pendulum for confirmation before I continued to the next one.

Whenever I found one who didn't go Home I'd write down his or her number and return later to them. I did this for each and every one of the four and a half thousand and in the end, after about three days doing this work, I was left with about 450 who still remained. I went looking for reasons why they were not going Home, and it wasn't too long before I found my answers. Some had lost a family member and didn't want to move on until they were found and the spirit knew they were safe; another had a strong connection to the land that was holding them back; and others felt their behaviour during the Famine made them unworthy of getting into heaven.

I whittled away at those who were left till I eventually came down to one. This last one who needed to go Home was a priest who refused to go till he knew his flock was at peace after all the trauma he and they experienced during the Famine. That was simple enough to resolve: I got his congregation to come to the gates and allow him to see they were OK. With that, he agreed to go Home and all were at peace. My commitment to the 4,500 spirits had been fulfilled – maybe a little late – but I had done what was asked of me and learned a lot in the process.

One evening almost a year later, Pam and I finished a workshop and went out to our favourite place on the island, Keem Bay. We parked the car and looked out to the sea. We had planned to stay there a while but within a moment I said to Pam, 'I don't know what it is, but we have to get out of here now.' I felt a real sense of discomfort bordering on fear. She said she had the same feeling, so we turned the car around. On the way back to the house Pam said, 'I know we will be OK when we go past the second little bridge on the road after the hill that leads to Keem Bay.'

When we got back to the house we called in a lot of protection for the two of us. After doing that we didn't feel afraid and I was told by Spirit that the next day we would be fully aware of why this happened and what we had to do.

We awoke the next morning and after we got up I was told by Spirit to go to the lake on Achill known to me as the corrie lake. It was near to where we had got the premonition the night before. The lake acted as a reservoir on Achill, providing water for the local community. Spirit advised me not to take Pam with me as she might be at risk. It was unusual for me to do spiritual work without Pam but I had to do things the way Spirit wanted. Though I was now rarely afraid of spirits and energies, I did feel a bit anxious. Calling in protection again, I felt reassured. I trusted then that whatever I was to do would work out OK. It was the first time I had to work like this on my own, and was a pointer as to how I would work in the future. Spirit was showing me that I didn't need someone to hold my hand. It was like I was a big boy now.

Upon arriving up at the lake, I said my prayer, which involved calling in God, Christ and Archangel Michael. I stood in silence and in the trust of God and waited to be told what to do. The message was not long in coming. *You have to release 5,000 spirits and you must complete your task over the next three nights before the time of the full moon.* OK, they had given me a job to do, and they had learned from the last time to put a time limit on it!

Needless to say I challenged this. After all, I had just recently sent back 4,500 spirits. Were there really that many more? I was then reminded of how old Achill was and also informed that some of the spirits involved in this new task were elementals, from the fairy kingdom. This made it clear why Pam was not to come. She had been energetically attacked before on a sacred site, whereas my leprechaun energy was able to cope far better with the naughty side of the elemental kingdom. I know how crazy this sounds, but just because it sounds crazy doesn't mean it's not the truth.

When I got back to the house I told Pam about what had happened. While I had been out she had looked up some texts in an Achill history book and it was then that I found out that the area around the lake used to be called the Valley of the Fairies. She also discovered that the second bridge she talked about the night before was on a boundary of the infamous Captain Boycott's land. It transpired that back then any animal which crossed the boundary onto his land was killed. Also, in the late 1800s the land was fertilised by seaweed taken from the shore and carried up the hill by local workers. It was very hard work for the people who were only paid a pittance for their toil.

I set to work to help the 5,000 spirits release their ties with Earth and go to heaven. I lit a candle, did the opening prayer and started, checking as before that each one went Home before I did the prayer for the next one. Because it was such a long-drawn-out process, as I progressed through the numbers I got a bit 'sing-songy'. The more bored I got the more sing-songy I became. However, I was determined to finish this job promptly and to stay awake throughout this process.

A couple of nights later I was woken up at about three o'clock in the morning, and was told to go and look at *Sky News* on the TV. Breaking news showed a terrible earthquake in Haiti, and on the footage you could see a beautiful little girl being pulled from the rubble. This young child was laughing and hugging and kissing those who rescued her. She was full of life. It left a lovely warm feeling in my heart as I went back to bed. But when I woke up the next morning and turned on the news I heard that the poor child had died. Archangel Michael spoke to me and said, *Remember who you are praying for and helping to go Home, so have some respect.* In truth, I never meant to show a lack of respect, but I have to admit I should have treated what I was doing with more sacredness. I got the message.

One day I was drawn to take a visit to the deserted village at the foot of Sliabh Mór. As I walked on this historic land I looked down the road and suddenly it was like I was caught in a time warp. I saw the area as it was two hundred years ago, and watched as men, women and children headed back up to the village with their animals. They were laughing and joking as they went. The vision lasted only for a moment. It was an incredible experience, and so clear it was like looking at a scene in a movie.

Sometimes in life we can feel sorry for ourselves, and we should acknowledge the pain we are in. However, we should never let the pain dominate us. As I looked at the deserted village I realised that it was now just part of history, and no one escapes history. Each generation carries their own woundings and trauma. I have had a good deal of trauma in my life but I never starved, always slept in a comfortable bed, and experienced a lot of love and good times too.

Spirit asked me to help 300 go Home from this village, sternly reminding me that it was only through Spirit's help that I would be able to do this. I was more or less being told again to be respectful at all times when doing this sacred work. Again I proceeded with a prayer of protection, cut ties with anything that might be holding them and said the prayer to release them. As always, there were a few stragglers, but eventually they all went Home.

Occasionally, during gateway work around the country, spirits would ask me to say the prayers in Irish. I am not a native Irish speaker so had to translate the prayers in my head from English to Irish as best I could and then speak them out loud. I think that sometimes they just wanted to have fun with me and make me squirm. But I have to say when I spoke in Irish I felt I was honouring my Celtic tradition, spirituality and heritage.

Since I started doing this work I have worked with lots of

different spirits, sending them Home and helping them find peace. I am fully aware that all is in divine timing and that no spirit is lost. God in His infinite love and mercy cares for us all and holds us safely in the palm of His hand until we are ready to go back Home. Once we see God in this way we can release the fear and let go of separation. When we do that fully, going back to God is a joy.

∽

I don't know what God looks like or what colour, sex or size He or She is. (By the way, I say 'He' because I find it's the easiest way to refer to Him, probably because it was the way I was conditioned). But I do know God is omnipresent. Did God need me to send spirits Home? Absolutely not. He gave me a job and asked me to take responsibility for it, and I do try. Do I do it well enough? Probably not, but whatever shortcomings I have I do believe God will ultimately make things turn out the way they should.

Mediumship has always been a struggle for me. I have talked to lots of spirits down the years, but find it very hard to see myself as a medium. Spirits speak to me, that is true, but it's usually when I least expect it and it's on their terms, not mine. I'm not in control. I cannot promise the person talking to me will get the information they want from Spirit, but I do believe that they will be given what they need.

It is not up to me to provide a permanent link to those who have passed, as we have to let our deceased loved ones go so we can focus on our own lives. Life is for the living and human beings need to grieve, but don't need to stay trapped in grief. The other side try to help us in the struggles we encounter in our daily lives, including dealing with the sense of loss we feel when we lose someone precious to us. All of us in heaven and earth are inextricably linked and always will be. There is nothing to be afraid of in spirit and when you believe and ask for protection, then you will be protected. I eventually learned to trust protection, and that gave me the strength and courage not to live in my natural fear of the unknown. Your own energy will tell you when you need to ask for help, but don't ask in fear; ask in hope and faith.

Down the years I have had some magic moments talking to spirits – sometimes sad moments, sometimes happy, sometimes funny. I have met some lovely people in spirit with great personalities, and have no doubt that they still love the family and friends they left behind. Sometimes when a loved one or family member goes Home we forget their human-ness, and that they had a personality at all. Be assured they are just as quirky and funny on the other side of life as they were here. But they are no longer sick, no longer struggling, and no longer addicted.

For all of us living in the physical world, rest assured that there is a very real connection with all the loved ones who have passed into Spirit, and the love we shared transcends the grave.

From my experience, forgiveness forms part of healing. It is clear we all get it wrong at times and our deceased loved ones now know what mistakes they made when on earth. Some are also aware that back in their human form there were times when they created real hurts to others. They never want us to hold onto any pain about them after they pass over and long for us to find healing and peace. They also want us to know that it is time to let go of our own bad behaviours towards them, which could include guilt, resentment and regrets. When measured in terms of a life shared, the pain falls into insignificance and the best memories remain. Where they are now, they don't hold onto anything other than the love they shared. When we make peace with our deceased loved ones we are able to love them freely and ourselves more. It must be understood that forgiveness is a journey, not a destination, and each person comes to forgiveness in their own time. For those who suffered horrendous pain at the hands of someone who should have loved and protected them, they may only come to forgive truly on the other side of life, where there will be full understanding.

Going through my own healing has helped me come to terms with the deaths in my family. My dad was first, and the hurt and the pain associated with his passing probably precipitated my healing journey. Then my brother Joey was next. Unbeknownst to me, he encouraged me to go past his house on the morning of his death to avoid all the drama. Then I heard a voice in the car which told me I'd go home to find out something I wouldn't like and to get on with life. It became clear later that this was Joey's spirit talking to me. After that, there was the feeling of utter peace I felt when my brother John took a massive heart attack on his way to St Michael's hospital in Dun Laoghaire and died, and later Marcus sent me a message of elation as he was freed from his pain as an alcoholic. Finally, Kevin gave me the privilege of working with him through his passing. Not a day goes by that I don't miss them, and I still keep their memories in my heart. I feel a real sense of peace now because I know for sure they are all fine, and I will meet them again when it is my time to cross over.

I have not a doubt in the world that when animals die, their spirits, like humans, live on and grace heaven like they graced Earth. The loss of a beloved pet can be a huge tragedy and it warms me to know that we will meet our non-human companions again, just like we will meet our own loved ones, when we pass over.

Down the years in my work with clients I have communicated with a small number of animals who want to impart messages to those they loved while here on earth. When I was living at home with my wife and children, we owned a Jack Russell terrier. Her name was Mini, a cheeky little dog, and she was with us for many years. We all loved her and she was a real gift to the family. After Mini died my daughter Sarah saw the little dog several times standing at her bedroom door looking in at her.

No matter what kind of spirit it is and how long it might have remained earthbound, it eventually always ends up passing through the gates of heaven to love and light and the real happiness of being Home where all their loved ones are waiting patiently to welcome them back. The links broken on Earth are reunited in heaven.

CHAPTER 17

Reflections • More Achill Adventures

Pam and I had to keep lots of balls in the air and it was difficult, as it was just the two of us trying to maintain and develop the centre. We had to produce a high turnover to service our debts, and I constantly had to keep a close eye on the financial situation, which was always volatile. But at least on moving to Achill we were starting to get traction again, and it looked like we would finally be able to feel a bit more secure. Had times been different, had we had less debt and more working capital, it may have all worked out the way we wanted. I feel for Pam in this regard. As one businessman put it, 'I'd rather be lucky than good', and we were not lucky.

Ireland as a country was in a real state of flux. The world had changed, credit was being squeezed and people no longer had the same disposable income they used to have. However, in believing all was as it should be and trusting in the divine plan, we had to walk our own paths and trust things would turn out OK in the end.

I cannot deny I had matured a lot and I realised that sometimes in life we have to accept we can't control everything. It was strange, though. The harder we tried to get things right the more things seemed to go against us. Sometimes it was as if a negative invisible force was trying to block the light.

Sometimes Pam and I did talk about the threat of darkness to the twin flames, because we knew there would be attacks on us. Where there is light there is also darkness. Examples of this included the random event of the car being broken into outside the shop. In that attack, the darkness was represented by those who broke into the car, and the light was the fact that we were protected by Spirit in that the thieves left behind the most valuable pieces of equipment we needed for the operation of the aura camera.

There were also people who were jealous of the twin flames and who wanted to begrudge us and put us down. This darkness in people comes when they don't believe in themselves, and then feel they need to slight other people. On the opposite side, we met many wonderful, caring and supportive earth angels along our journey. We were often wrecked and our bodies did suffer a lot energetically and physically from the work we were doing, but we constantly reminded ourselves that the light always wins.

To regret the adventures we had on Achill or decisions we made back then would be churlish. God in His infinite wisdom had brought us together, and the fruits of that journey can be seen now, many years later. For the most part I have ridden the storm and am grateful for the awakening of my spirit. If I had done things differently, I probably would not have learned or grown as much, because despite all my losses I have gained a lot. I feel it is better to take risks and in so doing learn and grow. I could use this analogy: ships in the harbour are safe, but they aren't made to stay close to the shore. If trust, faith and courage were enough, Pam and I would have succeeded beyond our wildest expectations. We certainly have positively touched many people's lives since 2003 and in that sense I feel blessed. Personally, I found my life purpose and learned to trust and value life more. I have learned to be still and know that God is in charge, and He has helped me through the raging torrent.

Achill had the advantage of being a very spiritual place, somewhere you could find sacred space and leave the world behind for a while. Pam and I wanted to let everyone know how wonderful it was, and what a positive and healing experience it would be to visit the healing centre and explore the island, walk the beaches, and be amongst the beautiful hills in this almost timeless setting.

During my time in Achill, I got to know many people in the community. I joined in on sessions in the local pub with a group of men and women who played there on Friday nights. It was a privilege and very pleasant. Their music reminded me of my involvement with Irish music and dancing when I was a child. Pam occasionally visited the pub and tapped her feet to the music, but for the most part, this was my thing. The first gift I got from Pam when we were brought together in 2003 was a top quality low D tin whistle. It meant a lot to me as it was clear she was thinking about me. That was the tin whistle I played at my brother's funeral. I also played the tin whistle on Achill at a more light-hearted event. The local school, Scoil Acla, applied to the *Guinness World Records* to break the record for playing the one tune on the most tin whistles together. I joined them on the beach as they all played the tune, '*Fáinne Geal an Lae*' (Dawning of the Day), during a big festival of music and learning on the island. And yes, we broke the record!

Spirit was always walking with us and now and again they would show us they were present. One night, while watching *Bridget Jones' Diary* on the telly, I was told by Spirit to get Pam to draw a Star of David on my back with her Egyptian oils. She groaned a bit but complied. After a while I drifted off to sleep. When I awoke the film was over and a documentary was being broadcast. I couldn't believe it when I saw it was about a young woman, a descendant of a Nazi leader who travelled to Australia to apologise to a descendant of a survivor of the concentration camps during World War Two. This demonstrated to me that healing is happening in many different ways all over the world today, and this spiritual truth can show our connections to others in the strangest of ways. It was also becoming clear I had strong links with the Egyptian oils, the Star of David and concentration camps, and these connections were to come up time and time again on my journey in the future.

One thing I avoided on Achill was the annual Christmas swim. Every Christmas morning a group of brave women and men head into the cold waters of the Atlantic for a quick dip or swim. They may think it is refreshing – I am sure for them it is – but it is not for me. Despite coming from a place on the east coast with two harbours, I never learned to swim – thank God!

One night, after a busy week of training, Pam and I were told to drive to the top of the hill that overlooks Keem beach. As we sat in the dark, wondering why we were there, we were told to keep waiting and watching. Then we looked up in the sky and appearing before our eyes was a beautiful display of the northern lights, the aurora borealis. There we were, twin flames sitting together and watching our own private light show on a seemingly deserted part of the island. Another gift from God.

The owner of the house we rented also had a tiny shepherd cottage on the Atlantic Drive. One evening she met us and talked to us about meditation. I suggested that her cottage might be a nice place for her to meditate in. Pam came back with the idea that I could meditate from there with the owner. I wasn't totally into the idea of going there, but found myself agreeing all the same. So a few days later the owner and myself travelled to the lonely cottage overlooking the sea. We were followed by curious and (to me) sinister-looking sheep, who actually came all the way into the cottage after us. The woman had to chase them back out!

As we sat down and meditated, I received a vision of the sea giving up her dead. It was like the sea opened up its graves, and I saw spirits dressed in what they would have worn when they died. As they walked in from the sea, it was a bit like looking at a collection of characters from a fancy dress party. A number of months later a friend of ours, Peter, who also lived on the island, said he had seen something similar around that time. He had also been sitting in meditation and perceived this phenomenon in his mind's eye while looking down from his home high up on the side of Sliabh Mór. He put this amazing incident down to tectonic plates moving under the ocean. This was as a result of a small earthquake (registered by seismologists) that had occurred off the western coast a little before he saw this vision. When the earth is disturbed it seems to release trapped energies, which is part of what Mother Earth does to heal and cleanse herself.

This shows us that there is purpose in everything that happens in nature. As you look through different eyes, you can see that every natural event on earth has a purpose that leads to renewal and rebirth, and is part of the integrated miracle of earth's creation.

One day, while placing crystals around a local house on Achill for protection of the home, I was called by Spirit to place some more crystals in marshland a few feet away from the dwelling. This was not to be done that day but two weeks later. After I went back at the appointed time and completed the task, I returned home to find out that Pam by chance had been talking earlier that day with a historian from the area. He confirmed that the place where I was doing the spiritual work was directly in line with a village called Newport in County Mayo where a priest had been captured and hanged in 1799. He added that a mural still existed of the execution on a wall in Newport. The historian also confirmed that some of the people responsible for the execution were ancestors of the Browne family. I knew the Browne name was popular in that part of the west of Ireland, and that they had got up to a lot of mischief under British rule, but I didn't know one of our lot was responsible in any way for the execution of the priest.

When I gave it more thought, it made perfect sense that I was now healing my family tree. Browne is quite a common name and with such a large family my ancestors were able to get themselves into a lot of trouble historically. This brought me into doing a lot of land healing work all along the west coast of Ireland. I guess it was all part of healing my own ancestral heritage, but the frequent reccurrence of the name became a bit frustrating at times.-

Financial stress and pressures were always with us and each month I was trying to get more and more out of less and less. The challenge of trying to survive was eating into our world and the spiritual wonder and joy that should have been ours. My dad used to always say that money was the root of all evil. I'm not sure I agree with that but certainly lack and the fear of lack was a weapon that darkness used against us.

The reason I talk about this now is because it was here Pam and I started to really lose each other. I was meant to be happy to be on Achill. I wasn't. I was meant to be happy to surrender to divine providence. I wasn't. I know I should have been grateful for the wonderful journey and the amazing spiritual experiences I had, but there had been so much negativity, pain and hurt in the journey of the twin flames that this was impossible. I was grateful, though, when my children came to visit me, and they really did lift my spirits.

First to arrive were my two sons, Liam and Eoin and Liam's

girlfriend. I had joked that because the place was rural they would need rubber boots. They took me at my word and came down wearing psychedelic boots of different colours and styles. When I brought them to the local pub, the regulars there sized them up and branded them good-naturedly as tourists straight away. We all had a great laugh and enjoyed our time catching up with each other over the next few days. It meant so much to me that they drove all that way to see me, but nearly broke my heart when they had to go back home.

Then my two girls also came to visit. It was great to see my precious ladies, but again heartbreaking to see them go. Things like this were constant reminders of what I'd lost. My children are the most important part of my world. Like all kids they have their moments, but the light they brought into my life, and still do to this day, cannot be measured. Each one of them, unique in their own way, have filled my life with treasured memories. However, because of my spiritual journey I was not able to be there for some of their growing-up years and will always be sad about those lost times. Strangely, having to separate from my family helped me to understand my father more, and to realise that life is just life and you cannot control it.

The place where I once felt I really belonged was no longer home to me and now whenever I visit Dublin I feel like a visitor. As a younger man I loved the sight of the River Liffey as I returned from my trips down the country. Now my place of residence was Achill, so far removed from Dublin's hustle and bustle, the city lights, and my own roots. I was locked in Pam's world, not mine, with all the pain of feeling homeless.

Writing this book has given me the opportunity to reflect

on the many challenges we had. It was a time of tremendous conflict. I was definitely the vocal one, and Pam objected about issues in a quieter way. Sometimes the arguments between us came from differently held and equally valid views. If both us couldn't agree on something, one of us would have to compromise and I began to see that I gave way more than I should have done.

Living with Pam was like having your own therapist on tap as she constantly fed me back wrong or hurtful things I might have said. The intention for the two of us coming together was to do the work God wanted us to do, but it wasn't easy to feel united or equal when I was constantly under the microscope. Every statement was analysed, every word had underlying meanings. Although Pam and I were both continually working on our self-development, Pam had been at work on herself far longer than I had, and I felt she was in a more evolved and superior place than I was. Now I can see more clearly. I can see that over time Pam's feedback actually eroded my self-confidence and made me question the forty-four years of life and learning I had before meeting her.

Sometimes we can have awareness but we also need to understand what is in someone's heart. Being a bad communicator does not necessarily make you a bad person and sometimes we do use words carelessly. It was hard with Pam for she saw meanings in what I said that were not in my heart. On the one hand it made me more responsible and aware of the words I spoke, but it also created separation rather than unity. I found myself realising that I dishonoured my own history in overly honouring Pam's. I forgot the basic truth that God brought us together as equals, and possibly this was my biggest mistake.

I understand it is easy to blame the therapist. Maybe I expected too much from Pam – she had human needs and a right to the type of life she wanted, and maybe on a human level she wanted more than I could give. We were just two human beings struggling against a lot of obstacles.

'

CHAPTER 18

Trouble in Paradise

'The weather in Achill is no worse than Dublin, no wetter or stormier.' This was Pam's claim, but it never felt that way to me. I always thought the east coast of Ireland had a much better climate than the west, but then in November and December 2009 the weather across the whole country took a nosedive.

Bad weather had been forecast by the Met Office, but I don't think anyone could have imagined how bad things would really get. First, Ireland was deluged with rain, and flooded roads were widespread. Driving conditions were appalling, and attendance at the holistic shows suffered as a result. We still went to them but the small numbers of people attending was evidence they didn't want to venture out from their warm fires unless absolutely necessary. Who could blame them? Then in December and January we were treated to the coldest weather and some of the worst snowfalls in the last three decades. The roads became skating rinks at times, and we took our lives in our hands every time we went on a trip.

Around October I came up with the idea of offering a three-day promotion and sale of our crystals in selected angel shops, and knew that December would be the ideal time for this adventure as it would help support our turnover during a quiet month. We decided to bring our wares to angel shops in Sligo, Tuam and Limerick, and to our relief this turned out very well. Along with receiving much-needed income, the shops benefitted by expanding their range and sales of crystals for Christmas. We continued working with these stores in this way for about two more years.

Time is slightly blurry around then as to the exact time when events occurred, but I do remember the dates we had booked for the Sligo angel shop happened to be just when frost, ice and snow came to visit. Our margins were so tight we could not justify staying in a hotel and so I drove there and back every evening. Pam stayed at home during those particular days, and I was helped by a wonderful friend of ours who accompanied me on these trips. The roads were like glass everywhere. On one of the days, as I carefully drove between the town of Tubbercurry and Sligo, we saw an abandoned car lying perched precariously on top of a wall. I can just thank God that we didn't end up the same way. Anyhow, we survived and our visit to Sligo worked after a fashion. It was not big money but welcome all the same.

With tremendous help from the same friend who came to Sligo with me, we did a holistic show in Slane during the Winter Solstice. I didn't want to do it because I felt it was too late in the year and too far to travel, but taking chances at this stage was better than having nothing to live on. It was here I was about to start to learn non-attachment to the physical things of this life.

Pam and I were always used to buying crystals before a big show, but because of the economic climate, we couldn't do that now. We had to depend on the stock we had, and sell our personal crystal collection as well. Over time we had collected a few special crystals on our trips to England. They included an incredible collection of clear calcite that looked like mountain ranges, and two Herkimer diamond quartz crystal twins, one with two clear diamonds and one with a citrine diamond. They were really beautiful. Also in the collection was an amazing citrine point that Pam had given me as a gift some years previously. It was a beautiful golden colour, the same hue as my soul bottle.

At the Slane show one of the twin Herkimers broke, leaving the beautiful citrine diamond separate from its twin. As things turned out, this particular piece sold at a good price, and it headed back to New York where it had come from originally. I guess it just wanted to visit Ireland for a while! We were very grateful to be able to sell the crystals, so all in all it was a good show, well worth attending. We drove back to Achill on appalling roads for Christmas, tired but happy.

My good friend and helper took a beautiful photograph of Achill as we left the island one wintry day and headed for Sligo. The resulting picture showed a pink sunrise over snow-adorned mountains and a glassy lake. It was amazing and it captured the changing beauty and magic of Achill in one splendid moment.

Pam went away after Christmas that year to visit some of her family overseas and I drove on treacherously icy roads over to Dublin to leave her to the airport. Luckily the runways were clear and the planes were able to take off safely. Needless to say, I was pretty tired by the time I got back to Achill on the same icy motorways.

So it had been another tough year for the twin flames. But good things were happening as well. Two of the standing orders we had hanging over us for a while were now completed and we had paid back nearly three-quarters of the loan we had on the black car. Also, at a Mind Body Spirit show we attended in Cork we launched our own little newspaper to let people know what we were doing on Achill. It helped us to fill two weeks of summer school, an inner child workshop, and brought us a number of new clients. If we could only continue holding it together . . .

We had our work cut out for us, as the recession was still gripping the country and people in general were spending very little. The Celtic Tiger (Ireland's economic boom) had at this stage curled up in a ball and gone to sleep.

We decided that since we could not afford to run two cars at that point in time, we would stop using the black car, and so we left it sitting on its hunkers outside the front door. It was a short-term decision that was to be a much longer one than first envisaged. We had never considered the damage the salt air and exposure to the elements would do to the car, and as weeks turned into months, the condition of the car deteriorated.

Using just one car meant one of us was stuck at home. To be honest, neither of us really minded, or so I thought at the time, as there was always something to be done around the house. But later, I would find out to my surprise that Pam felt abandoned and neglected whenever I went away to work.

One day, while I was at home, pottering around the place, I looked out the kitchen window and saw a Spanish soldier in full armour holding a long lance and marching nonchalantly past the front gate. Because he walked so slowly I had time to see he really was a spirit. It was just another one of the strange events I happened to experience every now and again, and these things could happen anywhere, anytime. It was a gentle reminder from Spirit that they were always present and that we needed to relax and all would be OK.

Around that time the owner gave us access to the rest of the outhouse. We were delighted about this, and spent time transforming it into an office. Because of the extra space we were now given, we could have a proper office and could prepare and organise everything for shows and other occasions more easily and efficiently than ever before.

During one of our days together on Achill Pam took me to see an old quartz mine that was nearby. When we reached the spot I was struck by the incredible energy that emanated from it. Apparently, when the road to Keem was being built, a lot of amethyst, a form of quartz, was unearthed. This could be another reason why Achill has such lovely pure energy.

The labyrinth we made became very popular, with several people coming into our garden just to walk on it. It provided a place of meditation and pilgrimage for many travellers, and we were delighted because that was what it was there for.

Whenever we had time we took trips to the sea and the beaches of Achill. It was always beautiful to drive around the Atlantic coast. During one summer a friend of ours was leading a Tai Chi session as part of a festival that was taking place on the Atlantic Drive, and Pam and I decided to join in. I had heard about this gentle Chinese martial art some years before, and was told it was very beneficial. But that day, when I tried to practise it, I found myself incapable of balancing on one leg for very long. Everyone around me, and myself, ended up in tears of laughter at my inability to do the postures. This was one of the many fun times I remember from back then on the island.

Life is never all bad or all good, it's just life, and with all the challenges we were used to having, we were prepared for nearly anything. However, we were not expecting the next challenge Spirit put before us. All of a sudden, just as quickly as we moved into the house on Achill, we were told we had to go. The owner was just as upset as Pam and I, but at least we were given three months' notice. She had a very genuine reason for us having to leave, but it didn't make things any easier.

When Pam rang to tell me the news I could hear the dismay in her voice. I was away that day but I will always remember how sad she sounded. We had to start packing and looking for a new place to base the centre. It was a very worrying time and I was frustrated that all the perceived promises of support from God did not seem to be materialising. We were trying so hard to make things work and just when things were slowly getting back on an even keel, this happened. It all seemed so cruel and unfair. I was very upset to see Pam this low as she was generally not someone who felt sorry for herself.

It took a few weeks before the dust settled and we could think about moving forward. While looking around for another place, we had to get started on packing up all our things. We had just finished setting up our new office, and now we had to take it all apart again. I did wonder if it would ever stop raining. It seemed there was always going to be something tripping us up.

Pam had told me the importance of doing your own work was that you could be more present for your clients. You would not hear what they were saying if you had your own stuff in the way. Maybe that applied to both of us. I kept preaching the divine gospel of discontent about living on Achill and the inability to work from this location, whereas Pam countered with: 'You're not living out of your new spirituality. Let go and let God.' Pam's words translated to me as, 'I'm not going anywhere. This is your lot, and don't be annoyed about it.' Her need to live on Achill and end her days there were more important than anything else, and it became clear that my options were limited.

But I had surrendered. I had moved to Achill. I had lost a lot and worked really hard and still the perceived promise of abundance had not arrived. Looking back I can see that a huge inner alchemy had actually taken place. No longer was I placing other people on pedestals, no longer was I accepting that I could not find a way of life on my own. My relationship with God and Spirit was mine and only mine, and He and I would have to sort this out together.

I was committed to the divine mission, doing God's work, but living like a hermit on an island wasn't fulfilling for me. I suggested moving closer to Castlebar, but Pam said there was no way that was happening. In fairness to her, she was entitled to be where she wanted to be and living together hadn't turned out to be as much fun as she thought it would be.

A constant reminder of the financial bind we were in was that the once beautiful black goddess which had cost us so much money and worry was now lying immovable outside our house. It accurately reflected how I felt then – beached and run aground.

We did try to compromise and eventually divine providence brought us to a house in Dooniver, a really nice little community on another part of Achill. I know that Pam was pleased to find somewhere to live on the island. However, I was not convinced that moving to Dooniver was a good idea. It was further into the island than our previous house, and would again add to costs whenever we had to drive any distance.

Since Pam's stress was so severe at that time, I hoped maybe this house could provide her with the security she needed. In signing the contract with Pam, she pointed out that this was the first house we signed for together. To her this was a sign of equality between us, but for me it was just surrender.

We hoped this would be our last move. The friends who had helped us with all our previous removals came to the rescue again and helped us move everything to Dooniver. We were very grateful to them for their generosity and kindness. I have to say it was a fine house with reasonable rent. We were given a small loan from a great personal friend to help carry us through that time, and still worked hard to make ends meet. We knew we had to put everything into God's hands, and hoped that things would improve.

I had compassion for the pain Pam was in. She was frightened and insecure, and so was I. It was all very difficult.

CHAPTER 19

Searching for Peace

This newest house provided plenty of space for us to set up our healing centre. A large room in a converted attic was going to be ideal for healing, training and meeting spaces, and the owner of the house told us that a gardener would cut the lawns outside whenever needed. The room was not going to be ready, though, for a few weeks after we moved in. The owner was in the middle of installing a new staircase and was also renovating part of the upstairs.

We were very pleased with the downstairs living room, which had a great view of the sea, and sometimes we were lucky enough to see dolphins swimming and playing in the distance. We also had a garage with an attic where we could store the contents of the print room and various other bits and pieces we had accumulated over the years. An extra blessing was that we had some really nice neighbours.

On our first day there, two of the neighbours came down. The husband introduced himself and his wife and welcomed us with a bottle of wine. While we were moving in another little visitor came calling as well. The builders, who were putting in the staircase, saw him too. Every morning, as soon as the door was opened, he was in like a shot. Gradually, this beautiful tabby kitten nosed his way into our lives. He was so cute and clever, and a welcome joy to our chaotic lives.

Because the black car had seized, we had to get it moved down to our new home in Dooniver by a local mechanic. As a result of the ongoing recession, it had ended up being parked outside the house for nearly a year. Our intention was to get it up and running at some stage, in spite of its current condition, as it wasn't that old and should have had plenty of driving life left in it.

I was starting to develop healing clinics around the country, and that meant I was working on my own a lot more. In the early days Pam was not in favour of the twin flames doing healing clinics outside of Dublin or working separately, but things had changed over time and she didn't object any more. Up until now our healing centre had been too far away for many people, but with the establishment of clinics in locations across Ireland, that problem was greatly resolved. Few people still came to Achill but our outreach programme was working. The Dublin clinic was already up and running, and Limerick and Tralee clinics were soon to follow.

These trips took me away a lot from Dooniver, leaving Pam living alone. I now understand how hard and lonely it must have been for her, but in those days I tended to have tunnel vision and in this regard I wasn't able to see things from her point of view. As far as I was concerned, it was a fight for financial survival, and because of the high costs associated with living on Achill we were always fighting against the odds. No longer did I see a living spirituality as the avoidance of doing the best you could in the physical world.

Living in Dooniver was like living in a different world. We had to drag the bins up a good length of lane when we wanted them collected, as the bin lorries could not get close to where we lived. We got our nameplate on the gate and put a letterbox on the gatepost, and waited patiently for the room upstairs to be finished, but typical of the journey on Achill it seemed to drag on and on. Deadlines came and went, and our stress levels began to rise again.

Little by little the tabby kitten, now named Whiskers, worked his way into our lives. Pam had a soft heart and allowed the feline to stay. He eventually grew into a lovely cat, and it was amazing to see him creating certain spaces in the house for himself where he could rest and sleep and make himself at home. He was a bit bossy but that made us love him even more. Later, we found out that Whiskers's owners lived next door and we were relieved to discover they didn't mind that the cat had adopted us.

Pam and I continued to work hard and tried to be as positive and pro-active as we could, but the delay in getting the room ready upstairs didn't help our humours. Furthermore, the weekly travelling we still did to shows was taking its toll. It was no fun loading up the car at 5 or 6 o'clock on cold wet wintry mornings, setting up everything at the venue (which took about two hours), working for the entire day, packing up everything again and then driving the long journey home. Pam did a lot of the drives home, which I was grateful for. All in all, we did our best to hold everything together.

In Ireland we get a lot of rain, but not a lot of snow or sub-zero temperatures. At the end of 2010 Ireland was battered by another terrible winter of rain and snow. I have been driving the roads in this country for many years and can safely say the worst weather I ever experienced were in those two winters of 2009 and 2010, during the time I lived on Achill.

I had planned a three-day visit to Limerick to work with crystals in an angel shop there. It was to be my last event before Christmas. The weather was fine during my visit, but when I set off in the car to go back to Achill I got as far as the Limerick road to Claregalway when it started to pelt snow. By the time I reached Claregalway the roads were white – in fact, the snow was falling so heavily the roads were becoming impassable. As it was too dangerous to travel any further I booked into a little hotel and hoped that by the following morning the weather would have improved a bit. But when I pulled back the curtains early the next day I was greeted by a snowy vista that looked straight out of a scene from a Christmas card. As I could not afford to stay in the hotel another day I hitched up the reindeer and crawled towards home on what should have been a two-hour drive. It actually took the guts of eight hours. As I drove I dearly hoped the conditions around Achill were better than where I was. Bad as the roads were from Claregalway to Castlebar, the roads out and around Achill were going to be far worse, because they wouldn't be gritted. I did hope there was a chance of Achill avoiding the very worst of the snow as in cold weather coasts are generally a little warmer than inland areas.

Progress along the roads was very slow, and the first place I got into difficulty was on the hill out of Castlebar and onto the Newport road. The car started to slip down the hill, which was a pretty hairy experience, especially as cars were coming up behind me. We were all like Bambi on ice. This road never seemed so long and high in normal Irish weather! Thankfully I got back up the hill safely, and onto the main road to Achill. When I finally arrived near the island, to my dismay I saw it was covered in snow, and I realised my treacherous journey wasn't over yet.

The next hill I had to negotiate was just off the main road from Achill Sound to Keel. It was a steep enough hill with bends winding down onto a narrow, fairly straight typical bog road. On the way down the car kept sliding from side to side until, unbelievably, it eventually landed safely at the end of the hill. Angels must have been helping me because I had little or no control of the car on the way down the hill.

Then I had two options to get to the house: One route involved going up another small incline, and the other was to drive along a flatter road that was narrow and had deep ditches on either side. I took the incline. Wrong option. I got to the top and then the car slid sideways down. Just when I was wondering how on earth I could get the car turned around the right way, some lovely people from Achill appeared and helped me turn the car around. I was able to drive on the flatter road and eventually arrived back at the house in Dooniver, exhausted but relieved to be home safely. My work was over for that year, and I was definitely not going anywhere till the snow went away.

When the great explorers of the world embarked on their perilous journeys, it was not the arduous conditions they faced that mattered the most; it was that they triumphantly arrived at their destination. The journey of the twin flames was like that. I learned to put all my faith and trust in God and I knew He would make sense of it all. Faith was the only thing I had left to hang onto.

It was hard to see Pam in any way upset, worried or under threat, and I also worried that I might have been too forceful in trying to get her to see the problems we were facing. Our stress levels became worse, and Pam's health during this time was not good. One day I saw her collapse in the kitchen and I got a terrible shock. For a few moments I thought I had lost her. A friend helped me to get her to bed and I called the doctor. It turned out she had a bad infection, and needed lots of rest. Thankfully, she recovered in a relatively short time. That is something I have always been really amazed at – Pam's incredible ability to bounce back from the many ailments and illnesses she had along the way.

I knew I could not keep everything going on my own so I invited some of those closest to Pam and me to talk about working together. I was willing to accept we could expand the schedule and let people coming on courses hear different voices along with our own. As a little group, we had an exploratory meeting in Dublin which I felt went really well. I was open and honest with the people there and told them what I thought. It would not be an employer/employee situation; we would be individuals working together.

There was a real doubt, however, among certain quarters whether or not we could work as a team. Their efforts of course would have to be paid for as the work expanded. I suggested taking a much bigger stand at the Mind Body Spirit show, and the cost would be shared relative to the space each healer or therapist took. Our extra members would create their own income from their part of the stand, thus giving them their earnings from the show, and leaving Pam and I with the earnings we would normally have.

However, Pam wanted to add all the income together and share it equally. The thing was, we relied heavily on the crystals and the camera income to pay our bills. We could not afford to share it; we could not survive if we did so. I thought I was being fair, but Pam thought I was not working in a spirit of community and co-operation. I felt I was being practical and maybe, under different circumstances, I would have agreed with her. But for now the survival of what we had been working on was more important, and we had to be realistic and prudent. At any rate, the meeting ended with us all agreeing to work as a team, and we organised a few events to see if this new collaboration could be successful.

The first event we decided to run together as a group was a spiritual weekend. It was part of an attempt to work closer with each other. Pam's ethos was that we were all equal, master and student. Both Pam and myself had always picked Aura-Soma bottles and angel cards together with people attending workshops, and anything we asked the participants to do we'd do it with them, honouring their equality. It was a fundamental part of what we believed and it was Pam who had taught me to honour people in this way. When I suggested that we hold onto this spirit of equality that Pam had taught me, one of our new facilitators responded in front of the group, with a verbal swipe, 'I will do it my way.' I felt firmly put in my box.

For Pam and me, it was not about hierarchy. It was about cherishing and respecting each individual and their unique gifts. I suppose for some the idea of spiritual leadership and superiority was more the tradition they came from and understood. This had not been Pam's way, or the way she taught me. At a time when I had finally succeeded in becoming more independent and taking responsibility for my own relationship with God, it looked like Pam's ethos had changed, choosing leadership over the idea that we are all in this together. It seemed to me that this was in direct contrast to her previous belief in equality and a shared divinity.

Someone once described spirituality as a stream flowing freely down a mountainside and religion being man's best attempt to bottle it. I deeply felt that what Pam had taught me originally was a real gift, allowing myself to embrace the equality of spirit of the human family, and so I was very surprised at this change in Pam. It was this change in direction that enabled her to support the inequality in the workshop and support the facilitator's point of view. From then on in, I stepped back and focused on the clinics, taking things day by day.

We continued working on getting the upstairs room done. But between one thing and another one day we had a serious disagreement about whether or not we would remain together. The discussion ended without resolution and we went away to different parts of the house to take a break. Later that same day, with tears in my eyes, I painted the walls of the large room and put the tiles down as well. I had no idea if I was building this for Pam or me. To be honest, I had no idea why I was doing any of this any more.

During that very stressful period of time I ended up in the garage twice with a rope around my neck. The first time it happened, it was when my frustration and anger had reached boiling point. I sat on the ladder in floods of tears, wondering where the trust had gone.

There had been considerable pressure on me to agree to do an Evening with Spirit night. Pam had also asked another psychic to come along and join forces with me during the evening. When this woman whom Pam had invited said she was unavailable we then agreed to let a gifted young man replace her so that he could gain some experience. However, due to unexpected events, the previously unavailable woman turned up on the night and expected us to change our plans for her. It was suggested that the young man should step aside, which was something I could not agree with. In the past Pam would not have agreed with this either as she believed that when you set out the intention for a workshop, Evening with Spirit or healing, Spirit starts to prepare the people for that event.

However, in this instance, Pam saw no reason why the woman could not join the young man and the rest of us in doing the Evening with Spirit. This was another moment when I had to hold my ground, so I didn't join in. That left the young man space to be there and experience the night. This was just another instance where I had to pay for the loss of Pam's support.

As I sat in the garage, I wondered where my place was in all of this. If I was always going to be pushed aside or be wrong all the time, then how could we ever make progress? I wrote a note expressing my sorrow at the isolation and abandonment I felt and planned to leave it behind for Pam to find. What helped me move away from my suicidal actions was the thought of the grief and hurt I would leave behind for my children and for Jean. I have no doubt if it were not for them I would have gone that night. I wasn't trying to create drama – I just wanted the pain and hurt to end.

The next time it happened was after Pam returned from a trip to Europe and came out with the statement, 'I'm not travelling around the country to do the camera any more.' That statement shocked me. We needed every euro we earned to service the debt we were carrying to just survive. The camera provided about a quarter of the monies coming in and it took two people to run it – and now this income seemed under threat from Pam.

I was really tired and snapped, 'We can't afford not to! We have to continue to do the camera and the shows. We need the revenue.'

Pam replied, 'Well, I'm not doing it.'

'OK,' I said, 'I'll have to get someone else to do it.'

'Who?' she asked.

'Anyone we can. We can't afford to lose the turnover.'

'You're going to replace me,' she claimed. I didn't mean this at all. I thought Pam would have understood where I was coming from, and that surely she realised we worked on many other things together as it stood. There was a time when we were able to talk to one another and work things out regarding paying bills and balancing books, but things were different now. Pam's behaviour showed she was choosing a different way of life regardless of what it cost.

That evening I felt I had enough. There was no way I could solve these unending problems and disagreements. I ended up back out in the garage with the rope around my neck for the second time. My thoughts were in utter turmoil. At this point I was working and fighting so hard for survival and Pam seemed once again determined to metaphorically tie my hands behind my back.

In that moment all the struggle and effort we'd been through seemed to be in vain. In an ideal world we would be financially well off, or maybe working as a charity, but we were neither of those. Also, Pam's need for a more ascetic type of life was not served by having to keep the centre going on an island with a population of just over two and a half thousand inhabitants. We needed to reach out to more people around the country. The commitments we had were high, but honestly these problems paled into insignificance when compared with the breakdown in communication between the two of us.

Everything I had was gone, all for a God that I had to trust. A God that brought me together with Pam, and then seemingly abandoned both of us. I was really angry. The hurt was enormous. I had tried against all the odds to earn enough to make the centre work, but now I felt like a slave. I was never going to enjoy this island, or Pam, any more. I was powerless. I had no future and no voice.

In that garage, I kept saying to myself, 'Just for today you do not have to die.' I kept repeating those words through my pain and loss. I didn't believe that I could come back from this dark place, but Spirit and my family – and those words – helped me survive. In those desperate moments I had to choose life or death. I chose life and let God do the rest. This has taught me to have compassion for anyone who passes this way.

There are many ways of ending our lives. As well as that, many people in our world today choose existing over living with the joy of experiencing the fulness of their being. This is a form of suicide. As they drift through life they let go of their gifts and dreams and hopes and build walls around themselves so that they can stay detached and safe and alone.

It's funny, when you have nothing left to lose, trust is actually easier, and as I started to let go of trying to fix things, I felt an unexpected level of peace coming back into my life, with a weight lifted off my shoulders.

Although part of me knew that things were meant to unfold the way they did, I still sometimes asked God: what is it all for? The only thing I could do was just keep going as best I could.

Around that time, on two occasions, I sat penniless in Dooniver, unable to go to the celebration of my nephew and niece's weddings. I was heartbroken. There were also other occasions when I really wanted to go up to Dublin when my children needed me, but could not afford to. I felt isolated and trapped.

I see now I could not blame Pam for what happened in my life. How could I? We both agreed to take this journey together and had to shoulder responsibility for the decisions we made along the way. But misunderstandings were the order of the day back then. We had huge inner conflicts and at times it seemed that both of us felt completely trapped in this situation.

I learned a lot during this time. I discovered I had my own courage, my own faith, my own will and no matter how hard things became, they were not going to be broken. I lived through many a dark night of the soul, having to dig deeper and deeper each time to find inner strength to help me survive. I know Pam was feeling like a victim, ruined by her twin flame. I too felt like a victim, who suffered because I let God into my life through Pam, wrongly believed she had all the answers, and that God would make it all work out the way I'd hoped.

Pam tried to support me to the end in her own way. We didn't hate each other. We had battled through too much for that. Survival is a natural instinct and that's where we were at in our lives. Decisions that Pam made then were more designed to wind down what we were doing rather than open up. She was tired, unwell, drained and needed to retreat into stillness. When we were based in Blackrock I had told her our vision of a creating a healing centre might not work. Back then she taught me to trust, and encouraged me to keep the show on the road. But now she had nothing left, and neither had I.

It would be wrong to give the impression that we were always fighting in Dooniver. We had some lovely moments there and even though both of us felt very alone at times, we did have better days. As I said already, Pam deserves credit for all she did. We were also very appreciative to have great support from good friends and neighbours.

CHAPTER 20

The Lighter Side of the Final Frontier

As I said, Dooniver was a nice house. We built another labyrinth and as with our previous dwelling, it had a beautiful backdrop of the island and sea. The inlet at the bottom of the garden which led to the Atlantic Ocean was just a stone's throw away and provided endlessly interesting views in the changing seasons. There was a beautiful little beach at the shoreline and when my kids came down they thoroughly enjoyed the stunning beauty around them and the clarity of the water which they would rarely see on the east coast. It was private, which made it even more attractive. The area around the house had a feeling of 'the road less travelled' about it, and the cul-de-sac we lived in was always peaceful. The only person we saw regularly was a local farmer, who would bring his cattle up and down the lane. He would always give us a wave as he passed by.

For the most part, Pam and I lived in this house like two friends who cared for one another. I was by now travelling a lot and far too tired to fight about anything when I came back to Dooniver. Because of this, the energy between us became a little more relaxed.

I felt spiritual energy was very high in this area, and one night I woke up in what seemed like a fantasy world. Flying around my head were stunningly beautiful little lights. They were a bit like miniature butterflies. It reminded me of the Tom and Jerry cartoons when Jerry would knock Tom out and you'd see stars circling around Tom's head. The lights were radiant colours of purple, pink, green and red and sparkled like tinsel or fireworks. I watched them twinkling above my head, amazed by their beauty. I could imagine my granddaughter being enraptured by them. It so happened that after a while I had to answer the call of nature, so I said to the lights, 'No, you're not allowed in the bathroom, so don't follow me.' When I came back to the bedroom I was sad to see the lights were gone. What they were I never found out, and can only be grateful to have experienced magic from an unseen world. I will never forget the gift of beauty they gave me.

I came to understand that these events were happening to support me through the turmoil. I was getting a tiny glimpse of another world and being shown that all I had to do was to trust that God would show the way. If the purpose of the twin flame journey was to reawaken my spirit to the spirit world, it certainly had been attained.

One day I received a phone call about a woman who had been threatened severely by a spirit. She was told by a healer that the spirit actually wanted to kill her. This sweeping claim gives spirits a bad name and did nothing for the healer who asserted this. I do not believe we should be afraid of spirits, but with comments like that it would be easy to generate fear. Ralph Waldo Emerson wrote, 'All fear is separation from God.' Hypothetically, if someone runs along a cliff edge and falls into the sea while chased by a spirit, this doesn't mean that the spirit caused him or her to fall. It is actually their fear, because the person is distracted by the spirit and isn't looking where they are going.

This particular matter involved house clearing, which is closely associated with land healing. It was an area I tried to avoid because of the high level of commitment needed. It is part of gateway work, but in general I tended to concentrate on spirits that came to me for help rather than carrying out spiritual cleansing on sacred or historical sites, where there would be a deeper complexity of energies to deal with. Nonetheless, this time I said, 'OK, God, 'I will do the work you are asking me to do.'

Very soon after I made my decision, seven books about land healing appeared out of the blue: they were randomly dropped into the house by people who had no idea I was interested in this subject but felt for some reason I should read these books. As it turned out, I never got the chance to work with that lady's issue, but I think the point of the exercise was to get me to commit to doing land healing, and to learn more about it. God does work in mysterious ways.

It took time to accept that there was a little bit of a leprechaun in me. Since many people in the healing world suggested that possibility to me, I didn't dismiss it out of hand. The usual representation of a leprechaun is a little man dressed in an

Aran jumper, with buckles on his shoes and wearing a green hat with a shamrock on it. As I am writing this, I'm thinking that no self-respecting leprechaun would actually dress like that nowadays and could even grumble that he is not here to entertain tourists!

One afternoon Pam started to read *Pilgrimage with the Leprechauns*, another book by Tanis Helliwell, whom I talked about earlier. It was one of the many books that came in the door to us. After a little while she started to giggle. This kept happening and eventually I asked what she was laughing at. She wouldn't tell me and said instead, 'You'll have to read it yourself.'

So I had to wait until she finished the book. To be honest, it was lovely to hear her laugh and be released from tension in those moments. Finally, she gave the book to me and as I read I saw what she was laughing at. All the mannerisms of leprechauns that were spoken of in the book – the grumpiness, the sarcastic wit, all of it – were evident in my personality at times. It was obvious on some level I was very like the fellow in that story, and I felt I could no longer doubt that I had elemental energy in me.

∞

Whiskers the cat was a natural-born hunter. He regularly took home a mouse, a rat or a bird to play with. One day, while sitting in the living room, we heard a thump thump thump nearby. When we went to investigate we saw that Whiskers was going up the stairs, carrying something large in his mouth.

Pam caught up with him and she saw it was a duck! There was a small pool beside the house and he had probably caught it there. The poor bird was dead, and she apologised to the cat as she took it away from him. 'Sorry, Whiskers, thanks for the gift, but we can't keep it!'

You also knew when you were in the cat's bad books. Whenever we returned from being away overnight he showed his disapproval by ignoring us. He wouldn't come near us unless we gave him a suitable treat. At best then we might get a grunt of approval – or was it disapproval? We might have to supplement the treat with an even nicer piece of food, and then he might let you give him a little pet. Two to three days later normal service was usually resumed, on Whiskers's terms. We really didn't have to worry too much about him being looked after. Whenever we were away Lord Charles could always depend on neighbours to look after him.

Whiskers entered and left the house whenever he felt like it. At night he regularly came to Pam's bedroom window and knocked on it to get in. This could happen at two or three in the morning! But that didn't matter to our Charles. It was really Pam's fault as she was too soft-hearted and always got up out of her bed to let him in.

One time Pam had to go off for the day and I was to hold a workshop in the house. Pam was always very organised and she had arranged for lunch to be brought in for the trainees. A local lady used to do the meals for us, and this time along with the main course a beautiful dessert with cream was included. Everything was left out on the table by the lady. During the morning's training I suddenly thought of the cat and what mischief he might be up to. Sure enough, when I went to check, there he was licking the cream off the dessert. You had to have eyes in the back of your head that with fellow.

∾

The abundant wildlife and domestic animals around and about continued to beguile and amuse me. Herons used to come and feed by the water's edge, and a hare used to frequently dart up and down the lane, checking all around as he ran to and fro. The next-door-neighbours had a dog called Molly, who often came to visit. She was very respectful and well-behaved, but would give a little growl if she thought we were not being affectionate enough to her, particularly when she made the effort to call over to us.

In the field next to us there were two red cows. They could be a bit off the wall at times. Regularly we saw one of the cows play-chasing with the farmer. When he ran to get her she would hop over the fence near his wall and run down the lane and back again until she and the farmer had enough. This reminded me of the sheep on Achill who avoided their farmer in the same way. They are all cleverer creatures than we give them credit for!

Pam liked donkeys ever since one sneakily nicked a lick of her ice cream on Achill when she was a child. I found out you could adopt a donkey from a sanctuary set up for these animals in Sligo. Pam was thrilled when we adopted a beautiful chocolate brown donkey called Dunphy who loved ginger nut biscuits. We'd go up every now and again to visit him. This was one of those times that I will always cherish.

∽

Pam loved to entertain and always liked to cook up a nice meal for our friends when they were invited to dinner. This didn't happen often enough for Pam, and was something she really enjoyed doing. A few very pleasant evenings were had as we sipped fine wine and ate good food.

The people of Achill are wonderfully generous, and a lovely couple of ladies often dropped turf down to our garage. We were always grateful to them for doing this. Another example of Achill kindness was when I arrived back home from my eight-hour drive in the ice and snow in the Christmas of 2010. I saw a friend of ours had parked at our house in his big four by four. He had called down to find out if Pam needed anything. It was an honour to be included in this caring community, even for a short while.

Pam helped organise a holistic festival on Achill in conjunction with Achill Tourism and other healers on the island. The main event was held in the local community centre but other healers' houses, including our own centre, were used for some of the events. Achill Tourism greatly helped out in promoting the festival by giving details of the satellite locations of healers' houses and scheduled events from their office in the Sound and on their website. All in all, it was a wonderful celebration of Spirit at work on the island.

One evening I was watching *Crimecall* on TV and there was a report about people robbing oil from oil tanks around the country. I suggested to Pam that it would be an idea to get a lock for our domestic oil tank. Pam said, 'We don't need to worry about that on Achill.' Believe it or not, very soon after that programme was broadcast, someone stole oil from our tank. We moved the tank inside the garage after that, and made sure to keep the door locked at all times.

∽

There are lots of things I am happy with in this life, and working for God, even though it cost me a lot, is something I would not change. My experience with Pam made me stronger and helped me to rebalance myself and accept my gifts. I know now that communication is crucially important. It is essential both to listen and speak. Living with Pam was a huge learning experience. Her dedication to duty and her absolute determination to serve was something I wanted to emulate. Even after everything that went wrong, I began to really like and trust people. She also made me realise that you should never put people on pedestals, because they can only come tumbling off them.

I believe that God is the conductor of the orchestra and therefore I accept He brought me to where I needed to be until it was time for my journey on Achill to come to an end. I was also learning self-reliance and fortitude, and to 'Let go and let God'.

CHAPTER 21

Coming to the End

With one car off the road, Pam was trapped on the island when I was working away. The clinics were growing slowly: two days in Dublin, one day in Cork, one day Tralee, two days in Limerick and one day in Galway. That was seven days out of the month. A number of crystal exhibitions took even more days away. This meant Pam and I were together less and less. When I got home from my faraway trips Pam would often have a special meal cooked for me, but because I was often preoccupied with problems I didn't always receive this caring kindness as well as I should have.

However, we did still work together. We had the aura system in operation and travelled to Ennis and Limerick to do readings there. We also went to Cork with the camera and crystals, and held training weekends on Achill. Added to that, Pam did some educational contract work from home.

Things should have been easier moneywise but weren't. It was at this time in utter frustration that Pam asked me, 'Do

I live to work or work to live?' I thought for a moment and answered, 'Live to work.' I am not sure, however, that this was true. We just had so much to do, always. And there were times when I was absolutely exhausted. I never experienced this before, where literally I could not do any more and at the end of a long day I just lay on my bed, zombie-like. I found myself blaming Pam and then blaming myself for getting into this mess. Sometimes I even blamed God. The truth was, I just felt helpless with the whole situation. I was like the boy who put his finger in a dike to stop a leak. There was a happy ending for him, but when I stopped the water flowing in one hole another leak always seemed to spring up somewhere else.

I always said we'd earn more money doing any other work – even if the job was at a fast-food diner – than the work we did in the spiritual world. But I began to understand that both abundance and lack are a state of mind, and that has been a very valuable lesson through all of this. There was no doubting how hard we worked, and just like Pam I felt really unappreciated at times. I can see that we felt we were victims of each other, but the reality was we were victims of an ideology. God said, 'Man can't live on bread alone,' but He never said man does not need bread to live.

All any of us can do is the best we can and trust that God will guide and bless the outcome. It can't be successful if it doesn't come from the integration of our physical and spiritual beings, as our decisions need to find sustenance for our mind, body and spirit. When we do that, we find enthusiasm and the god within ourselves. We enjoy the power in action and learn to surrender and trust as long as what we do comes from the heart.

Anything I tried to do had a basis in logic and was about building for the future. When I look back, I feel I could have given more attention to Pam on so many different levels, and could have protected her better. But behind all of what I saw and felt as chaos and betrayal, God was in His heaven and everything was right with the world.

Twin flames are brought together to teach each other or awaken in each other their gifts and talents. Some are destined to stay together while others are not, completing the rest of their earthly journey separately in their new awakened state. Pam and I got a chance to live and work together and it became clear over time that both of us were meant to eventually go in different directions, despite what I had initially felt regarding what God had promised us. I had been resistant to change and had fought like hell against it. You'd think I'd know it was all about surrender and trust at this stage, but the only view that mattered here was God's view.

I know now this was the way it was meant to be. Over in Dublin God had successfully put my family in a safe place, and the kids were getting on with their lives. I was pleased that Jean was enjoying the experience of being a granny for the first time, and I was also delighted to become a grandad. Pam had already created her own support structure that would continue after we separated, and she would always have good friends around her. The way it turned out, a new space in life would also be created for me.

Nearly nine years of battling had left me unemployable in anything other that what I was doing. My energy ran so high that anything which involved working with computers was out and furthermore, who would employ a fifty-four-year-old man? Also, I had no money and was in horrendous debt, not just the debt associated with Pam. I had borrowings on my credit card and the credit union, and stock still had to be paid for.

At that point we were in all the main holistic shows in the country with the camera and the crystals, but Pam's thinking had changed and she started to make clear moves to distance herself from any joint positions.

In hindsight we possibly could have created more business through the Internet but honestly I didn't have the skillset or knowledge to do it and could not afford to buy in the right people to help make that work. But now I know it would have worked if it was meant to be. In all the intensity and stress this eager beaver was spending his life trying to push a rock up a hill without realising that this was not what God ultimately wanted. He wanted me to recognise that He was in charge, and that I should relax and let Him guide me whatever way He desired.

As I struggled to build the clinics I felt I was just going through the motions. My brain kept thinking about what to do next, but by and large it was done with little heart. I still tried to make better decisions, one being reducing the size of our stands at the main shows to save money. This was done at the right time and funnily enough, we managed to gain profits from the shows as a result. But because of the economic climate at the time, overall trade at the bigger shows was nose-diving and eventually the main organisers pulled out. This resulted in the major shows gradually closing down over a three-year period.

By now the clinics had grown to two days in Dublin, two days in Cork, two days in Tralee, two days in Limerick and two days in Galway. Ten days per month. They were starting to bring in income, and I was quite used to doing them by myself at this point in time. It was just as well Pam wasn't joining me now because it would have put too much pressure on her physically. I was ten years younger and even I found it very tough going. I understand and accept now it was all part of God's plan.

Preparation work was underway for a change but I didn't know that yet. The endless driving was a killer, and the work was hard. Ultimately the only real joy I had was in the progress the clients made, and the privilege of doing the work.

At 2 o'clock in the wee hours of a Saturday morning, I was driving through Kilcolgan, near Galway, on my way home from Cork, when a brick flew off the back of a truck and hit my windscreen. I got a terrible fright and pulled in on the side of the road. In assessing the damage I saw the brick had left a small hole in the windscreen. If the glass had completely given way things could have been so much worse.

In that very moment I decided that I'd had enough. I'd rather be dead than continue to work and live in this way. It was crazy, this endless driving morning, noon and night. I also considered all the hotel expenses and the cost of the cars and thought: maybe Pam and I could rent a cheap house in a town like Ennis. I could stay in it overnight and not have to go all the way back to Achill, driving so late. It would save the costs of hotels and I could possibly use the place as a clinic as well, which meant it could pay for itself. It all really came down to the fact that I could not cope any more with the way things currently were.

As I resumed driving I really wasn't surprised when I saw the engine management light on the dashboard flash on and off intermittently. Just one more thing to worry about. The car I was driving was the same make as the black car which was laid up in Dooniver, and I worried that this car now had the same turbo problem. Every time it came on my heart raced faster as I awaited the car's possible demise. After what seemed like an eternity I arrived back to Achill safely. The car was definitely down to the mechanic the next day, but before I dealt with that I had to have a conversation with Pam.

At breakfast the next morning I told her my thoughts about a rented house, and how it could save money, but the way she heard it was that I was leaving her. Up to this point I was still in denial about what should have been obvious to me by then, but now Pam's words drove things home. I said nothing back to her at the time because I was trying to process what was happening. We didn't pursue the subject any further right then, but knew we had to sort the matter out sooner rather than later.

Within a week Pam had come up with a plan which signalled the end of us working and living together. She would borrow a small amount of money and get me a cheap second-hand car to replace the one I had that was now starting to cause problems. Pam said she would drive my car, as in the main she would only be travelling locally, while she waited to get the black car fixed and back on the road. This way we would have a working car each. She also told me I should take what was left of the crystals along with my clinics and she would keep the camera and hold the workshops on her own. It was agreed that we would continue to teach Reiki together for the time being. The split of the healing centre's assets comprised of a third to me and two thirds to Pam, which included the ability to create income based on historical sales up that point. The debt would be split the same way. And it was taken for granted that Whiskers the cat would remain on Achill with Pam.

We would then work together to find a house for me from where I could more easily drive to all the clinics. It really was the beginning of the end.

Regarding the search for my new home, first I thought about going back to Longford, but it was a little too high up in the country. Then there was Mullingar, but that town was where Jean and I had bought our first house when we got married. It would bring back too many memories. Maybe Athlone? It was central, but a bit awkward to get to from some of the places where I had clinics. Then *Ennis* was shouted in my ear, the place I had thought of initially. It did seem to be the most balanced location-wise, as most of the clinics I had set up were along the west coast of the country. I was still unsure, so did what I knew was the best thing – I asked God. The answer came back as a definite *Yes* for Ennis, with the extra knowledge that this location had been already planned by Him for some time.

From a business point of view the arrangements regarding the share of the materials in the healing centre seemed fair, but emotionally it was something I never wanted to happen. Pam also gave me her old set of Aura-Soma bottles. I pleaded with her not to do this till her work and mine got more settled and secure but she would not agree to that. It was a very sad day when it dawned on me that this really was the end. Pam had her Achill, and for the moment I had nothing but trust and faith.

As luck would have it, the following week we had a show in Donegal and the crystal stand produced enough money for me to rent a small house in Ennis. I found myself in a state of shock because things were moving so fast, but Pam seemed quite relieved. Around that same time she asked me to do an inner child workshop with one of her friends. I said I could only do one day of it as I was working on the Sunday. To be honest I really didn't want to help out at all but felt I could not refuse outright.

Pam and I found a little house very quickly and I made the move to Ennis. So it was finally over. Pam was in Achill on her own, and I was in Ennis on my own.

Just before I left Achill, I was passing the stand with the bottles. As I glanced at them, one of the bottles winked at me. It was Bottle Number 65: Head in the Heaven, Feet on the Earth. No, I was not going to check out the meaning for this bottle, I argued with myself. I was too fed up and tired and angry. But after a while curiosity got the better of me and I looked it up. The line that jumped out at me was, 'You think you're more important than you are.'

What a thump to get in the head after all I've done, and after all I've lost. And now I am told all my efforts didn't matter at all. I was reminded of a film called *Trading Places*, where two rich brothers played games with the lives of two people, destroying one and exalting the other. With me, God was the puppeteer and I was the puppet. I had given up my family, my friends, everything I had and maybe it was all for nothing!

I was beside myself with anger for a few days. On the third day, when all good resurrections happen, I was given a vision of a little child from somewhere in the far east digging through rubbish for his dinner, and I heard, *What makes you more important than him?* I got the message. It's just a journey. Everyone has one and we all have our own stuff to deal with.

Pam already had many life experiences of letting go and moving on under her belt and was used to starting again. This time her faith and trust would take her through stormy waters to a more calm and measured place, and eventually would see her re-emerge in service and community. I would have to keep going; there was no option. God made sure of that. And any feelings I had about having failed were my own. God was about to show me my life was absolutely not over, and that He can turn anything around.

My dad used to say, 'It's a long road that has no turning.' When we were first brought together as twin flames I had picked an angel card in the Angel Shop in Dun Laoghaire. The card I chose was St Brigid. My mother and grandmother's name was Brigid, and the card carried a warning that the invitation to go on this journey was not going to take me to the place where I thought it would. This challenged me to release any misconceptions about the path ahead. However, when I moved to Achill I was sure I was going to live out the rest of my days there. Yet here God was, pointing me in a different direction and I had absolutely no idea where life would take me. In the end all I could do was surrender and trust and go along for the ride.

'If you have faith the size of a mustard seed . . .'

CHAPTER 22

A New Beginning

It is amazing how quickly life moves on when you let it. When I first considered renting a house in Ennis, it was never about moving from Achill or giving up on the twin flames and the work we had fought to do against all the odds for nine years. I had invested so much in the healing centre's eventual success, and given up all I had emotionally, physically and mentally, that I had found it almost impossible to let go. But now our journey together was finally ending.

It was interesting how we discovered my new home. Pam and I went down to Ennis to check out a few places, and realised quickly that there was really only one option. As we drove into a little cluster of houses, we could not but notice the colours on the walls of the house we were going to view. They were painted in gold, the colour of my soul bottle, and the edges of the walls were painted pink, the colour of Pam's soul bottle. The two colours together represented trust. The number on the house was eleven, and Pam and myself are both number eleven in numerology. When we went inside the house we saw a number of pictures of little angels and a Quan Yin lamp, the Chinese version of the divine mother. In her hands was a coral flower, which is regarded in some holistic circles as the colour of the new Christ ray. In Aura-Soma the colour coral is seen as love and wisdom and also brings healing to unrequited love. This absolutely mirrored the hurts I was feeling inside right then. In the back garden there was a ring of stones which, for me, represented a fairy ring, and two trees standing side by side like a number eleven. In the middle of the ring, just for good measure, was a little statue of a seated gnome. It was like he had been waiting there for me.

After settling the rental arrangements with the landlord, it seemed like no time passed before all my belongings were transported to Ennis. Pam and I said our goodbyes and off she went back to Achill. The many long drives I had to do to and from the island were over, as was the struggle between us.

I knew I had to trust, but also had to face the possibility I might not be able to pay the rent for the next month. My thoughts were still in turmoil. I felt pushed out and betrayed. For a time I felt all was lost, and yet I could not give up on God or myself. I had to keep going and do my best with what I had. But how was I going to fix all my debt problems, and how was Pam going to survive? I was concerned about her. She had to keep the figures up, and had to do lots she hadn't done before. As it transpired, Pam was able to reduce her workload and turnover, and started to work to live. She then went on to easily deal with new challenges and changes in her life in her own inimitable way.

The first thing I noticed in this new place, when things began to settle, was the peace of being alone. I could potter about in the house or go up the town, which had a decent population and was a hive of activity, with loads of shops, lanes and side streets to explore. I could also go out and play music at night if I wanted to. This was the first time I ever lived by myself. I was free. I could do what I wanted when I wanted. I had little need of Pam now, and missed her a lot less than I thought I would. And most importantly, I no longer wanted to die because it was easier for me now to choose life.

Little by little I sorted out my financial problems. The clinics continued to grow and I started to see clients in Ennis. In my day-to-day living I was bright and happy. I had a small telly for a while and even did some trainings on healing and crystals from my new home. I concentrated on finding myself again. I opened up my own bank account. Everything I had previously earned had gone into a shared bank account with Pam so there had been no need to have a separate account. Even though there wasn't much in my new account, I was happy that every cent I put into it would be mine, and I could manage it in my own way. My son then gave me an old telly he had, which had a good big screen. I also had a nice fire, nice food, the odd beer. I was sleeping again and my spirit was on the mend. Even heaven seemed to have given me a break and time to heal. Pam and I talked frequently on the phone, but just superficially.

Part of me, however, was still angry and sad. Deep inside I still felt my life had been moulded not by free will, but by unseen forces I had no power over. For a time God was definitely in my doghouse.

One day I was heading out to work in Limerick when I saw a little old lady struggling up the road with two bags of shopping. By the time I came up to her to offer her a hand, she had made it to her front door. She gave me a quick nod and a smile before she opened her door and went in.

As I continued on my way I thought, Aren't people amazing. Despite all the pain and hurt they feel, despite alcoholism and other addictions, abuse difficulties in the home, despite grief, guilt, blame, shame and sadness . . . despite all these things they get up and fight, not just some days, but every day. I talked to God and said: 'I will do as you ask of me for them, but it does not mean I am happy with You. You may still be my Master and I your servant, but I am not a happy camper. But I do want to work for them, for the countless people who feel traumatised by life and sometimes don't even know it. I also include those who are constantly suffering from physical pain, who through their courage and commitment overcome the most difficult of times, and are still able to be kind and loving. In the future I will only ever come from a place of Your love, even though our own relationship may take time to heal. I will be of service here to help people, God, not because I want to be cooperative, but because it was what I was made for, and I will do this till I finish this life.'

∾

Over time, things got a little easier for both Pam and myself. Her sense of peace restored, Pam regained her energy and drive and with help, the portion of debt she had started to diminish. Her health improved and our intrepid explorer was ready for her next journey. It hadn't been easy for us and even though I didn't know what the future would hold, bitterness or resentment was not part of my plan. For the rest of my life I will try to live out of the love of the twin flames, and the more gentle gifts of earlier times.

From all the events and upheavals in my life, I have retained my faith. I admit that trust and surrender still ebb and flow. Am I heading into a calm peaceful existence now, or just having a break? I don't know where life will take me in the future, but I'm sure it won't be boring.

I know Pam played her part in awakening me. It will be interesting to see what happens when we meet again on the other side. I also wonder what tomorrow will bring for this half of the twin flames. I think we both know we have a special connection that we will only truly understand when God calls us Home. I think, however, we'd both want to re-negotiate our contracts next time round. But it is truly hard to be ungrateful when I look at the balance of the events that brought me to where I am now.

In my new life I work about half a month, and try to rest and recover in the other half. I am not upset or stressed the way I used to be. Pam did me a favour in letting me go. I would have died on Achill, broken and burned out.

Eventually Pam decided to change direction and she gave the aura camera to her friend Trisha. Things really do work out in their own ways. I now know that I am free to live my own life and make my own decisions. Pam has no more influence on me, other than what she taught me, carefully measured against what God is telling me to do. I know that Pam would not want to hurt me in any way or me her. I cannot control her onward journey. I have no right to do that, and I know she won't dictate mine. I will now operate from here on in using my gifts fully for the benefit of my clients in this world and the next, and I will do it all by grace and guidance. I may not always get the right balance between spirituality and commercialism, but one thing I know for sure is that I will never give my power away again.

I am much happier these days regarding my connection with God. I understand so much more now. I try not to fear tomorrow, believing if God is with me, who can be against me? And I also accept that even when you trust, you can still go through tough times.

In the final analysis I'd wonder if anyone else going through the journey we were on would have come out of it unscathed. Since leaving Achill, I've used the gifts and knowledge I've developed and learned from my spiritual experiences as well as the skills I amassed in my ordinary working life. I have not compromised my deep faith in God or the love I have for Him. I know He'd never abandon me and is always there. As someone once said: 'Every day is a new life to a wise man.' In the darkest moments of my life I may have momentarily doubted His commitment to us, but in hindsight I know He is the Master of all.

I ask that in your reading of this book that you are kind to Pam and me. It was a tough journey, and in thinking we had finally failed we had actually succeeded. We completed the path we were meant to go on together, and with all we learned while working as a team we were now guided to embark on very different and individual paths from here on. Relationships are never easy, and we certainly had our challenges. However, I would not have been able to have started the journey without Pam's courage and strength, and I am still proud to call her my friend and twin flame today.

With all I have learned thus far, I know that every person who walks this earth faces challenges. Up to the age of forty-four I felt my victimhood quite intensely, but since awakening I really became aware of the suffering of others. As a result of this, I was able to see that people have a great capacity for compassion and love, as well as tremendous strength of character, courage and resilience. I see many individuals selflessly putting their lives on the line for others and feel honoured to be part of the human race.

In those times when we experience the dark night of the soul, when we doubt we can find our way through the pain, if we hold on just for a short time, life will do what it always does: it will change. In going through very difficult times I discovered a deep inner peace, courage and strength. I have completely put my life in God's hands in the knowledge that He will bring me to where He needs me to be. I'm not sure I would volunteer to come back to Earth again, but all the same I don't regret being here.

I am grateful to God for the light and the learning He gives me every day, which enables me to continue in service to Him. I also thank those people who played their part in the drama out of which so much light has come, and continues to do so.

True understanding of why we are here on this earth will only become clear when we pass into spirit. Till then let us forgive a little more each day, trust a little more each day, and surrender a little more each day, knowing we are human and need God to lean on and guide us as we travel on our own individual and unique paths.

ACKNOWLEDGEMENTS

I would like to thank Nicola Sedgwick for the tremendous work she has put into the editing and design of this book. Her care, craft and expertise has turned my hieroglyphics into a readable book, and has made it accessible to all. Nicola, I could not have done this without you.

I also want to thank God and the Holy Spirit for the mischievous activities which brought this book into being. I definitely spent a lot of the early years questioning whether or not I was a healer, and I reckon now I'll be questioning whether or not I am a writer for the next few years!